WORKING WITH INTERNATIONAL

STUDENTS AND SCHOLARS ON

AMERICAN CAMPUSES

edited by
David McIntire and Patricia Willer

National Association of Student Personnel Administrators, Inc.
1875 Connecticut Avenue, NW, Suite 418
Washington, D.C. 20009-5728
202/265-7500

**Library of Congress
Cataloging-in-Publication Data**
Working with international students and scholars on American campuses / David McIntire and Patricia Willer, editors.
    p.   cm.
    ISBN 0-931654-18-1
    1. Students, Foreign — United States. 2. College student development programs — United States. 3. Counseling in higher education — United States. I. McIntire, David. II. Willer, Patricia
LB2376.4.W67 1992   92-13340
378.1'9829 — dc20   CIP

Monograph Series Editorial Board 1991-92

Other Titles in the NASPA Monograph Series

Contents

Contributors

DAVID McINTIRE, Professor of Counseling Psychology, University of Missouri

PATRICIA WILLER, Director of International Services, University of South Carolina

WILLIAM R. BUTLER, Vice President for Student Affairs, University of Miami

JANET CONSTANTINIDES, Professor of English, University of Wyoming

WILLIAM K. CUMMINGS, Professor of Education, Harvard University

MURRAY M. DeARMOND, M.D., Director of Student Health Service, University of Arizona

PETER S. LEVITOV, Associate Dean of International Affairs, University of Nebraska

MARTIN LIMBIRD, Director of International Programs, Ball State University

CARMEN G. NEUBERGER, Dean of Educational Services, Dickinson College

JILLIAN HILLS STEVENSON, Assistant Director for Field Service, National Association for Foreign Student Affairs

TOM THIELEN, Vice President for Student Affairs, Iowa State University

Preface

The presence of international students in our colleges and universities is a major benefit to the American higher education system, providing campuses with the benefits of cultural diversity and pluralism. International students are invaluable resources on our campuses; they furnish the academy with an expanded and enlightened world view. They also present particular challenges because of their needs which must be met by both the student affairs and the academic sectors of our institutions.

An Overview
In this monograph, the authors examine some of the special conditions affecting international students and the particular needs they have within the American educational setting. It is their hope that the material covered here will assist student affairs and academic affairs professionals in their efforts to meet international students' needs.

Constantinides focuses on various academic issues as they relate to international students. She tells us that students from other countries who choose to study in the United States are, as a rule, both bright and highly motivated. The challenge and expense of international study are enormous and are usually not undertaken lightly. However, international students face some immense hurdles in adjusting to the American educational system.

DeArmond and Stevenson describe the challenge of providing culturally appropriate health care and counseling to international students. Traditionally, international students rely heavily upon campus health facilities and to a lesser degree on counseling services.

Levitov describes immigration law and discusses legal issues related to international students. The recruitment, admission, and maintenance of students, as well as employment, are highlighted in his chapter.

Butler examines the important topics of placement and re-entry. Just as student affairs professionals are concerned about the quality of the educational experience provided to students, they must also concern themselves with the fit between that educational experience and students' assumption of their postgraduate roles. It should be noted that the United States educates many of the world's leaders in government, business, industry, and education. Many institutions are becoming increasingly interested in developing alumni relations with their international graduates. It is also important to note that our international scholars are, to an ever-increasing extent, playing very important roles in the United States in the professions, and most especially as professors and researchers within our universities and colleges.

Neuberger highlights the many different areas of student affairs that are involved in meeting the unique needs of international students. She focuses on issues involving admissions, housing, and financial matters.

Thielen and Limbird address the important task for student affairs to integrate our international students into the mainstream of campus life. In addition to full integration into campus life, international students must be effectively incorporated in the life of the local community and state. International students can be very distinctive and noticeable within the greater community and it is imperative that their presence be viewed as positive. Thielen and Limbird suggest that to encourage positive feelings, the international campus should be presented as a cultural enricher and international visitors should be promoted as important resources.

Cummings describes the demographics of the international student population. He illustrates how the number of international students in the United States has grown so dramatically from the end of World War II through the 1970s. The 1980s realized only very small growth. If international student enrollment has stabilized, it is at a level where American institutions of higher education are educating great numbers of students from other lands.

The conclusion by Willer offers an assessment of our current status and prescriptive directions for the profession.

The authors hope this NASPA monograph will prove to be a useful resource. Improved understanding of the interrelations of working with international students on American campuses will enable educational administrators to do a better job with such an important segment of our student body.

Introduction

David McIntire

Throughout history, people have gravitated toward centers of learning throughout the world. Whether it was India or China 3,000 years ago, Greece and Rome or the Middle East during the Dark Ages, or Germany during the 19th century, students have always gone to places that were perceived as offering the best education in the world at that particular time. Although it would be difficult to assess whether the United States is offering the best in higher education in the world at this time, the United States has become and remains an especially popular place for international students to come and a very accessible place to find education. A combination of an available higher education system and a popular culture, with a relatively free lifestyle, makes the United States an appealing place for international students to seek higher education.

SIGNIFICANT CONTRIBUTIONS

When considering the contributions international students make to American higher education, it is common to speak eloquently about creating international brotherhood through contacts among people and the interchange of ideas. There is little doubt that, over the long run, the education of people from other countries has created goodwill for the United States. However, this is not to say that all international educational experiences are positive. Most international students and scholars, for example, never overcome their astonishment about the ignorance Americans arrogantly display about the world. Many international students diligently toil during their entire stay here to help Americans overcome this flaw in their national character. This is only one example of a quiet sort of contribution, while implicitly present, that is not readily quantifiable.

The benefits derived from the diversity that the presence of international students lends to the student body on a college and university campus are undeniable. International students are almost universally willing to talk about their home countries and regions, and they are well versed in their national histories and cultures. They are, in short, experts on foreign countries, regional cultural affairs, and foreign languages. As educational resources, therefore, they can be of immeasurable value to American campuses.

In graduate education, a high proportion of international students can be seen in technical and scientific academic departments. International students at many institutions make up more than half the graduate students in engineering, mathematics, chemistry, and often physics. They represent significant proportions of students in the biological sciences and other natural and agricultural science departments as well. Without international students in the graduate programs, many departments would not have teaching assistants to teach basic math, chemistry, physics, and engineering courses. Although this phenomenon waxes and wanes depending on the pay scales in private industry and academia, the pattern has been relatively consistent for the last 20 years in American higher education. Growing percentages of doctorates awarded in these fields are to international students according to *Summary Report 1988: Doctorate Recipients from United States Universities* (1989, pp. 6-10), and many of these students are now returning home after completing their degrees, as opposed to remaining in the United States, as was more common in the past.

Most higher education institutions consider the responsibility to help American students gain an awareness of international issues, cultural differences, and our country's role in the global community to be part of their institutional mission. As mentioned earlier, international students are a valuable and willing resource in these endeavors. Unfortunately they are underutilized, with their greatest effect being seen as a result of individual relationships and interactions between international and American students. Most colleges and universities have become far more adept at finding ways to make productive use of their international faculty and staff than international students in pursuing the educational goal of developing a global perspective for the campus. Some institutions, particularly those with extensive research missions, also consider world service to be part of the institutional mission. Therefore, the education of students from developing nations and the research that benefits those nations are crucial to the fulfillment of that mission.

The effect of the constant exchange of information and knowledge that has occurred throughout the world over the decades through visiting students and scholars is significant. According to Marcum (1988), the exchange of students and scholars between and among communist and noncommunist countries since the end of World War II (and especially during the late 1970s and '80s) has undoubtably contributed to the massive change which is occurring in many communist societies and there now exists a greater understanding of the intricate dynamics that generate peaceful change within a modern society.

Given the current state of economic affairs in higher education, it is becoming increasingly fashionable in the field of international student advising also to make note of the economic contributions international students make to their campuses and communities. Some rather detailed studies have been made outlining the fees paid and other living costs met by international students at particular universities or in particular states. Considering that international students generally pay the highest rate of fees at any university they might attend, it is readily apparent that their financial contributions to their institutions can easily outdistance those of any other identifiable group of students. For example, at the University of Missouri-Columbia,* approximately 1,000 of over 1,600 international students are enrolled full time and pay full-time fees. Thus, the institution collects approximately $5 million in fees each year from these students. Income from the fees of other international students (part-time enrollees, those with fee waivers, etc.) totals approximately $2 million per year. Therefore, payment of fees alone by international students at the University of Missouri reaches about $7 million each year. Each international student spends approximately $6,000-$7,000 per year in living expenses, totalling at least $10 million spent annually in the community. In short, $15 – $20 million are brought into the community and campus each year by international students, not including temporary visiting scholars and international staff working at the university. These monies are of great importance to the economic well-being of any campus, city, and state to which international students come in pursuit of education.

STUDENT AFFAIRS NEEDS OF
INTERNATIONAL STUDENTS

Duality of need is an apt description of the services international students require at higher education institutions. An international

---

*Special recognition is extended to Carl Leistner and Ginny Booker in the Division of Student Affairs at the University of Missouri-Columbia.

student services office can easily be characterized as a mini student affairs division, at least at colleges or universities enrolling several hundreds of international students from different countries. Contact with international student services often begins during or immediately after admission to the institution when I-20 forms (Certificate of Eligibility for Non-Immigrant Student Status) are sent to newly admitted students abroad, allowing them to obtain visas. The services continue with an orientation upon arrival and a responsibility to interpret the American educational system to international students continuously during their stay on campus.

International student services offices often have responsibility for administering financial aid programs, monitoring the financial problems international students experience, and assisting them with solutions. While only some international student services offices have direct responsibility for professional counseling, all international services include personal, family, and academic advising. Although international student services offices do not usually provide housing, they are often involved in international students' housing and board problems on campus and in the community.

Another important function of an effective international student services office is to keep its national and regional international student organizations as healthy and viable as possible. International students, unlike most American students, have a ready reference group available to them when they arrive on their U.S. campuses and these groups support their incoming fellow citizens. Without such assistance, an institution enrolling international students would either have to devote a much larger commitment of resources to its international student population or expect a high level of stress and distress within that group. Programming international student activities is very important, but significantly more complex and time consuming than programming for native students because international students engage in a much more participatory process than do their American counterparts.

Finally, international student services offices spend time assisting international students in relating to the community in which their college or university is located. Churches, service organizations, schools, and other groups in the community are very involved with international students. International student advisers, therefore, must understand and interact with the whole spectrum of student services, as well as being involved in the academic life of their students.

While some international students need more support than others, as a whole, they are an accomplished, mature, and goal-oriented group of people — from the 17-year-old Malaysian undergraduate to the 45-year-old Nigerian or Chinese. One need only to recall that every international student, unlike their American counterparts, is an international traveler and, in most cases, is at least bilingual. Many already hold responsible positions in the private or public sector in their countries and come to the United States with specific educational purposes.

Furthermore, the cultural gaps throughout the world are rapidly closing. The United States is known as a youth-oriented society and its youth culture is a prominent feature of the social dynamic. For better or worse, young people worldwide have gained both leisure and importance as the world has changed and developed over the past decades. With notable exceptions, young people worldwide dress alike and, with the availability of televisions, VCRs, and audio equipment, watch the same movies and listen to the same music. International students coming to the United States now must still make significant adjustments and some still suffer culture shock, yet the differences and adjustments to be made today are not as overwhelming for many international students as they were in years past.

Three fundamentally important differences between international and American students remain, however, and it is of great importance that faculty, staff, and student affairs professionals become more aware and sensitive to these differences. The first of these differences is legal. Most international student services offices spend over half their time and resources on assisting international students with their legal and other governmental obligations. All international students have some obligations they must fulfill with their own government while they are in the United States. Others have relationships with sponsoring agencies inside or outside the United States. More important, however, from the standpoint of international student services offices, all international students, faculty, and staff are subject to a complicated framework of regulations and policies put in place by the U.S. government. Complications and problems relating to that legal structure begin with the application for a visa abroad, and do not end until the international student or scholar leaves the country.

Furthermore, over the last decade the U.S. government has shifted significant responsibility for implementing its regulations for international students and monitoring their activities in this country to the educational institutions. On one hand, this shift in responsibility has benefitted everyone. Service is more localized and often faster than in former years when all applications and activities were submitted to the U.S. Immigration and Naturalization Service. Yet, many international student services offices are not adequately equipped to handle either the complexity or the volume of regulatory business these policies have generated. As a result, international student services offices have become more business-like and have been forced to retreat somewhat from promoting and implementing international education goals and activities.

Second, language proficiency still separates international students from American students. International student services offices are seldom directly involved in the delivery of intensive or supplemental English language programs. However, student advisers and others on campus who interact with international students must always be sensitive to language problems as a root of other difficulties these students may be experiencing. Whether academically or socially, international students will always be at a distinct disadvantage in an American educational setting due to language differences.

A third significant and unchanging difference relates to the financing of education. At public institutions, international students will always be considered nonresident and will, therefore, always be charged the highest rate of fees. International students are generally year-round residents in the educational community. These two factors combine to make the cost of education higher for international students than for American students. Some international students are from well-to-do families or receive some form of financial aid which finances their degree programs without significant difficulty. The vagaries of the international monetary system, however, always make the transfer of funds unpredictable at best and totally unreliable at worst. Given exchange rates and the length of some study programs, even the affluent in many foreign countries will have difficulty financing the high cost of American education for their children. Once begun, the consequences of failure in America for an international student are culturally and economically very expensive.

Finally, the flow of financial support to international students can be immediately terminated or seriously interrupted by phenomena unknown to Americans, such as political upheaval or natural disasters. In short, international students are financially at greater risk as a group than are Americans, and are much more dependent upon the understanding of their institutions when dealing with unforeseen changes in their economic circumstances.

Ideally, every faculty and staff member should have a sensitivity to and awareness of cultural diversity issues.

Realistically, however, many institutions could improve service to international students by at least making certain that, in each office, at least one person is readily available who is sensitive and skilled in assisting international students.

The number of international student advisers with degrees in education, counseling, or related disciplines has increased, a change from years past. Although a recent survey (Delancy, 1990) suggests that an educational background in business may be a means of entering the field. The question remains of how to better prepare student affairs professionals to work with international students. Many schools offer some coursework in cross-cultural communications and counseling and some provide internships or practicums in an international office for students expressing an interest in international education. However, there is still no coursework *per se* and certainly no degree program designed specifically for career preparation in international student advising. Yet, important qualifications exist. For example, cultural sensitivity is important in this field, certainly. A person who cannot respect other people and other cultures would not be able to function as an international student adviser.

Other skills fundamental to working successfully in international student advising can be acquired through formal education, including a knowledge and understanding of the American higher education system, and understanding major educational philosophies and systems throughout the world. A thorough understanding and tolerance of bureaucratic structures and procedures are also essential. A significant proportion of the daily work in any functioning international student services office is administrative. A great deal of time is spent explaining to international students about the "mechanics" of studying in the United States and living within the local campus and community environment. Obviously, the office must establish numerous procedures which produce the certifications, forms, and documents international students need to maintain legal status, qualify for and transfer money across national and international borders, arrange for and adjust to local housing, and maintain mental and physical health. Coursework in law and business, as well as cross-cultural communications, should be considered for inclusion in graduate preparation programs for those intending to enter the field of international student advising.

References

Delancy, J. (1990). Profiles, priorities of members emerge from NAFSA survey. *NAFSA Newsletter*, 41(3), 15-17. Washington, D.C.: Association of International Educators.

Marcum, J.A. (1988). Educational exchange: Reinforcing or challenging patterns of international relations. In J.M. Reid (Ed.), *Building the professional dimension of educational exchange* (pp. 25-33). Yarmouth, Maine: Intercultural Press.

Summary report 1988: Doctorate recipients from United States universities (1989). Washington, D.C.: National Academy Press.

CHAPTER ONE

Academic Challenges And Opportunities

Janet Constantinides

"Diversity is not to be just tolerated; it is to be sought as an enhancement of the educational system."

— *James Hurst, vice provost for student affairs, University of Wyoming*

International students who choose to study in U.S. institutions of higher education are usually among the brightest and most highly motivated of the student-age population in their home countries. The challenge of learning another language to a point adequate for pursuing university-level study, coupled with the expense of traveling to another country and the resultant dislocation, is accepted only by those students who have a high degree of motivation. That motivation may result from the fact that studying in the United States is viewed as prestigious in the home country or, in some cases, from the students' not being accepted to universities in their own countries and having then to look outside their home countries for educational opportunities (e.g., Japan and Korea). In either case, international students who arrive at a U.S. college or university have probably undergone a lengthier preparation and decision-making process than their American counterparts.

In spite of that, many international students arrive unaware of the immense hurdles in adjustment they must overcome to be successful in the American educational system. They have excelled as students in their own cultures, as evidenced by their having been in a university-preparation program, while many others in their country were excluded from such opportunities as early as age 6. They assume they will be successful in U.S. institutions. But cultural and educational system differences present new and difficult challenges. This chapter will investigate the academic challenges which are peculiar to international students, resulting as they do from differences in language and culture, and attempt to indicate how the results of those challenges may be exhibited to student affairs personnel.

ENGLISH LANGUAGE COMPETENCE

As obvious as it may seem, English language competence is at the base of the requirements for international students to succeed. It is important for student affairs personnel working with international students to understand that the level of language competence required to be a student in a postsecondary institution is very advanced. One way of viewing this is to think of language competence as having four levels:

■ Level 1: The "Good Morning, How Are You?" Level. At this level, the speaker can handle normal greetings and everyday general polite conversation.

■ Level 2: The "Let's Go to the Grocery Store" Level. At Level 2, the speaker can handle necessary functions such as shopping and dealing with tasks like having a telephone installed or having the lights turned on in an apartment or opening a bank account.

■ Level 3: The Student Level. This is the minimum level of competence for studying in another language, not just studying the language. The learner must be capable of being a student at the university level. This requires good listening comprehension skills and reading skills. Depending on students' majors, they may also require advanced writing skills, more so in the humanities than in the sciences, and advanced speaking skills. Because most undergraduate degree programs have some element of "general education" requirements included, an undergraduate student must be able to use all four skills with a high degree of proficiency. For graduate students, the specific skills needed will depend on the field of study. For example, math graduate students may not be required to do much writing in courses but will need writing skills to prepare a thesis or dissertation whereas political science majors will have heavy writing requirements throughout their studies.

■ Level 4: The Foreign Teaching Assistant (FTA) Level. This is the most advanced level and requires near-native facility. The student must be able to present information and material to undergraduates in a manner appropriate to a classroom, lab, discussion section, or problem/review session. Unlike the Student Level, which depends more heavily on the passive skills, i.e., reading and listening, the

FTA Level requires high proficiency in speaking and often in writing as well. Also, the level of listening comprehension needed is considerably higher than that of the Student Level because the FTA must be able to understand students easily to be an effective teaching assistant.

All too often, administrators, faculty, and staff fail to understand these different levels of proficiency. If prospective students write understandable letters asking for application materials (Level 2), it is assumed they have English proficiency adequate for being students (Level 3) or even FTAs (Level 4). Once the students are on campus, student affairs personnel may think the students can communicate because they have mastered Level 1 skills of polite conversation and assume that they will be successful students. However, a surface proficiency (i.e., Levels 1 and 2) masks a deficiency in language skills at other levels (i.e., Levels 3 and 4). Students may be able to manage the registration process, for example, or deal with housing personnel and the foreign student adviser's office personnel adequately, but may have great difficulty using the language skills at a proficiency level needed for being students. For example, students may be able to read course material with understanding but not at the rate of speed which is needed to be effective. Or, students may be able to understand short chunks of discourse, like those in conversation, but cannot "attend" (listen closely and with concentration) for 50 minutes to a lecture in English. If they miss a word or phrase, they stop attending to try to figure out that segment and, in the process, miss the next part of the lecture. When they can again attend to the lecturer, they are lost because they have missed information. An axiom quoted by teachers of English as a second language in American colleges and universities is: "Time spent now in studying English is time saved later."

Although it is sometimes difficult for both international students and their advisers or sponsors to recognize the truth of that axiom, it has been proven to be true. Students, and especially their sponsors, will protest that additional training in English is not necessary, that the students can function in English and should be allowed to enter and/or continue an academic program without any additional language training. Such protests are often made to student affairs personnel who need to realize and make clear that language proficiency is important, not just an unnecessary "barrier" placed in front of students. If students have only Level 2 proficiency and need to be operating at Level 3, the only chance of survival is for the students to spend an inordinate amount of time studying, probably reading and memorizing — thus becoming isolated from opportunities to interact in the larger academic and surrounding communities and thereby to improve oral English skills. Additionally, that studying may itself be counterproductive, depending on the strategies the students use, as explained below.

Therefore, institutions must have reasonable admission policies regarding English language proficiency. If an institution cannot offer additional English instruction after the student arrives, then it should set a high proficiency level for admissions to admit only those students whose English skills are already adequate for the demands of being a student. If, on the other hand, an institution can provide intensive or semi-intensive English instruction, then the admissions standard for language proficiency can be lower, but there should be mandatory testing and placement for incoming international students who then are required to take the English classes indicated.

Also, an institution should make it clear to prospective students when they apply and again when they are accepted that they may be required to take English classes upon arrival. Sometimes faculty and staff assume they are doing international students a favor by helping them bypass additional English instruction or by circumventing admission requirements regarding English. Usually such action is not to the benefit of the student. For example, a student who applied for graduate study in Animal Science was exempted from the English admission requirement because he had done undergraduate and graduate work in Mexico, had been a faculty member, and was "older than the average student." He arrived and began taking classes in a Ph.D. program. Within weeks, it became apparent that his chances of success were nonexistent because his listening comprehension and reading skills were far below the level necessary to follow his course. Try as he might, he could not maintain the pace of the courses in which he was enrolled. He left after a year, having spent his life savings to come to the United States. The department was unable to award him any financial aid because of his inability to maintain the required grade-point level. He returned to Mexico "in disgrace," having failed to receive a degree and with no money left to pursue any other course of study. Granting an exemption was no favor.

A source of helpful information about English language proficiency requirements and screening/placement testing is the intensive English language program, if there is one, or the English as a second language contact which may be located in the English Department. If an institution does not have an expert in matters relating to English as a second language, then it should consider getting outside expert advice in setting and enforcing admissions policies regarding English. The consultant service of the National Association for Foreign Student Affairs, the Organization of International Educators, is one source for such advice.

DIFFERENCES IN EDUCATIONAL SYSTEMS

Every culture has its own philosophy and purpose of education. From these are derived the expected behaviors of students and teachers in that educational system. International students coming to the United States, by virtue of their having succeeded in their own culture's educational system, have adapted to the expected student/teacher behaviors of that culture (Althen, 1981). As they enter this culture, they must recognize that there are differences in educational systems and how those differences will affect them. Student affairs personnel also need this information to effectively deal with students from other countries.

Status of Teachers

The status of teachers varies depending on the culture in which the teachers operate. For example, in Oriental cultures teachers command respect because of their position; it is not necessary for teachers to gain the respect of students because students automatically offer that respect. Additionally in Oriental cultures, the students' performance reflects on the teacher (Fieg & Blair, 1975). An Oriental student studying in this culture may not wish to discuss a less-than-adequate performance with "outsiders" (i.e., student affairs personnel) because of the negative reflection on the teacher. Students may assure the personnel that they are doing well in class, though grades do not support this. A common explanation for poor grades is, "I did not work hard enough," thus placing the blame on the student, not on the teacher. The real problem may be poor English skills, inadequate background preparation in the subject, or the student's lack of adjustment to the U.S. academic system.

In some cultures, again notably Oriental but also others, teachers act in an almost parental role. By accepting a student to study with them, they also assume responsibility for other facets of the student's life, a situation which the student accepts as normal. Thus, international graduate students may expect to confer with their advisers or professors about what would be considered in this culture as personal matters. For example, a faculty member in charge of a FTA course received a letter from a Chinese graduate assistant, begging the instructor to pass him. If the instructor did not, he wrote, he would lose his financial support and have no way to "feed my body and my soon to have child [pregnant] wife." In his view, this was appropriate behavior; as his mentor on teaching, the instructor should be concerned about his financial situation. Many American faculty would have been offended by the request since they would maintain that a student's grade should reflect only academic performance, not financial need. The instructor in question understood the reasons behind the student's writing the letter and, therefore, was not offended but did talk with the student about the inappropriateness of such a request in this culture.

Another effect of teachers being viewed as authority or parental figures is that international students may expect, based on their first culture, that they are supposed to wait for teachers to tell them what to do. Combined with the notion that teachers are the repository of truth (see the next section), this notion of authority gives teachers great power which American faculty may not realize the international student has attributed to them. In fact, they often misinterpret the students' "respect." Students may expect the professor to tell them exactly what courses to take, for example; but American faculty may expect students to make some of the choices. This difference in the expectation for who controls decision making is an especially big problem for many international graduate students. American graduate programs, especially doctoral programs, expect students to make many choices about the focus of the program, including the topic for research. But students may expect that such a decision rightly belongs to the professor. If students fail to make decisions about research topics, the faculty may interpret that behavior as lack of initiative and may not be willing to work with those students. The students will be confused because they think they have acted with great respect by asking the faculty to make the choice for them.

Purpose and Philosophy of Education

Another area in which differences among educational systems may cause problems for international students is the accepted purpose and philosophy of education in each culture (Henry, 1976). In most Middle Eastern cultures, for example, the purpose of education is to pass on the known "truths." The philosophy of education is that truth, being known, must be transmitted untainted to the next generation. Consequently, students view studying as the exact memorization of what has been written (Patai, 1983). To engage in activities which are considered normal modes of study in U.S. culture (i.e., rephrasing and summarizing) is considered inappropriate since to change in any way how the "truth" is stated could modify that truth.

The result of the international student's continuing to operate under this philosophy while a student in a U.S. institution may be an act of plagiarism in this culture: the student, used to the idea that what is written (what is in print) is the "truth" and should not be altered, will produce word for word, even including the punctuation marks, the information from a book on the theory that the written statement is the best statement of the truth and that a "mere student" should not tamper with it. In such a case, it is important for student affairs personnel and faculty to understand that the student's motivation was not to cheat but to present information in the most authoritative way possible, based on the student's prior experience.

These differences also affect the way students behave in the activities loosely termed as *studying* (Saville-Troike, 1976). In university-level classes in this country, students are expected to do a great deal of reading outside of class. In British English, the verb *read* is synonymous with study, i.e., "He is reading for a degree in _____." International students often find the amount of expected reading overpowering if not impossible. In part, this may be because the student's English reading skills are not adequate for the task. But it also results from having a differing idea of what "reading" is. For example, if the student comes from a culture in which reading is equated with memorizing short passages assigned each class period, the student may find the long reading assignments in American college-level classes overwhelming since the student assumes the material is to be memorized. The teacher, however, usually assumes the student will read the material, determine what is the important information, and remember only that, discarding the rest of the material.

Learning Style

A third difference often seen among educational systems of other cultures is the emphasis on cooperative learning. Students from Middle Eastern and African cultures may feel obligated to help a friend who is having difficulty in completing an academic task. In their cultures, the completion of the task by all students is given higher value than the correct completion of it by only a few (Parker, 1976). The American system, with its emphasis on individual performance and competition among students, sometimes allows students to work together, but only to a point. Beyond that point, any cooperative or collaborative effort is considered to be inappropriate, even cheating. For students who come from cultures in which cooperative/collaborative learning is the norm and the expectation, it may seem strange to them that they can be punished for working together. Recently, the University of Wyoming had a group of students from Saudi Arabia in a special program. They developed elaborate signaling systems for giving information to weak students during exams. They felt responsible for assuring that all students passed the exams. In fact, as they approached the qualifying exam which would determine who would remain in the program and who would have to return home, the better students wanted to know if the grades would be curved, an American grading concept which they learned about after their arrival here. If so, the best students had decided they would purposely not do well on the test to lower the curve so their friends at the lower end of the performance scale would not be sent home. Such "group responsibility" is not the expectation in the United States. In the worst-case scenario, the students might have been accused of cheating for not performing at the level of which they were capable. For them, however, the performance of the group was of more importance than that of individuals. They failed to realize they could have jeopardized their own places in the program, as well as those of the less abled students, by a performance on the test that was too low for a passing grade. In such cases, students need to be made aware of the extent to which cooperative/collaborative learning is accepted in this culture (e.g., study groups) and the point at which students must take responsibility for their own learning. For example, in science labs students may work in groups to perform an experiment, but each student may be expected to write a separate lab report.

Educational Systems

The organization of the educational experience in this country may be quite different from that to which international students are accustomed in their home countries, e.g., the semester/quarter system. Many other educational systems, especially those modeled on European systems, have year-long systems in which all students in a particular major take the same courses each year of study. Grades are based only on year-end exams. Under such a system, students may decide for themselves whether they are going to attend classes or do "homework" or practice problems which are not collected and graded. They often leave the working of problems/examples and the studying for exams until late in the academic year and then expect to have a period of intense study just prior to exams when no classes are held. They are unfamiliar with the idea of choosing their own courses, or having a series of graded tasks, either homework or exams, during a term which affects their grade in the course.

Many international students have had primarily essay examination questions for which they were given several hours to complete. They are completely unused to a "short" timed exam, e.g., 50 minutes. They have not learned to deal with the pressure of time in a testing situation.

Also, they are not familiar with and have not developed strategies for taking multiple-choice or short-answer tests or for solving problems in limited periods of time. Placed in a testing situation with a time-stress factor, many students find they do not perform well although they have always done very well in the testing formats used in their home countries. Again, reliance on those coping strategies which have worked in the past may cause great frustration. A Nigerian student, who had always scored among the very highest in every test he had ever taken, including a national exam for admission to a university in Nigeria, had developed a mode for test taking which involved spending 10 to 15 minutes getting ready, organizing his paper, pens, erasers. (In retrospect, he discovered that this was basically a stress-reduction technique.) When he had used it at the beginning of exams which lasted two to four hours, the time used in this fashion had not been a problem. But in a 50-minute exam, he was losing 20 percent or more of the exam time, leaving him inadequate time to finish. He was bewildered and depressed because the "safe" old ways, which worked well for him in the past, no longer worked. A similar situation occurred with a Cypriot student who had always spent time copying his exam papers neatly before submitting them. When he found that he did not have time to do that, he was distressed because he felt that handing in a "messy" paper would lower his grade. But when he allotted time to copy his exam neatly, he did not have enough time to finish the test. Relying on the strategies which had always served him well in the past put him in an unsolvable dilemma.

Another difference among educational systems is in the area of grading. In some cultures, there is a set grading system which is used for all classes. For example, in Greek universities for years it was the custom that all grading was based on a 10-point scale. Everyone in that culture understood that no student ever got a 10. The saying was, "Ten is for the professor; 9 is for the gods; 8 is for the best student." (This saying also provides insight into the status of professors in that culture.) A student who is used to such a system will have difficulty understanding grading scales that may vary from class to class and even from assignment to assignment within a class and what is a "good" performance on such scales. For example, if 80 percent on the scale above is considered very good, the student may assume that 80 percent in an American class is also very good, whereas it is possible that such a performance could be considered only average if the grades are curved. For a graduate student, an average or "C" grade is usually considered an inadequate if not failing grade. If international graduate students are not aware of that and proceed with the idea that they are doing well, they may find themselves in academic trouble — perhaps so severe that they cannot continue their studies.

Another problem resulting from differing expectations about grades is caused by the expectation of students from some cultures, notably those which operate on a "bargaining" principle, that grades may be negotiated. In Iran during the Shah's reign, university faculty were required to be in their offices for three days following the posting of grades to "discuss" grades with students. In fact, what happened was bargaining for grades. Both the teachers and students knew that was the expectation; consequently, teachers assigned the original grades with "room to bargain" built in. Iranian students in the United States found that the grades they received at the end of the term were not negotiable, but before they became aware of that fact they often had offended American faculty by attempting to use strategies for bargaining that had been successful in their home educational system.

Any philosophy of education implies certain appropriate actions on the part of students and teachers. For example, both the Middle Eastern and Oriental models mentioned above imply that the teacher, as the knower and transmitter of truth, is not to be questioned. The student's job is to learn, to memorize, to accept, to take in, but not to dispute, question, or challenge. Thus international students in American classes may be upset and uncomfortable with American students' propensity for asking questions, "arguing" with the teacher, challenging the teacher's authority. Of more importance here, perhaps, is the fact that international students may not be taking advantage of opportunities for learning, as they are perceived in this culture, because they do not ask questions. This may be interpreted by the teacher as indicating that a student is not preparing for class adequately, has not thought about or evaluated the material under study enough to be able to ask questions, or understands everything and therefore does not need to ask questions.

In addition, many international students use nonverbal communication, such as nodding, to cover the fact that they do not understand what is being said. Their lack of questioning often leads the teacher (or student affairs personnel) into thinking that the student understands what is being talked about when that is not at all the case. Further, in some American university courses, it is expected that students will discuss, debate, and challenge the material under study. To simply accept it, as lack of questions or discussion indicates to a teacher, could be interpreted as the student's failing to meet the requirements of the course. Additionally, in such a class, there may be no "right" answer, or there may be a variety of acceptable solutions. For students who are accustomed to the teacher giving the answer, it may be unsettling that the teacher does not indicate the right answer — these students may feel they are not in a position to make such decisions.

Furthermore, international students who come from highly authoritarian educational systems will expect that information, "truth," will come from the teacher. They, therefore, are not attuned to the idea that class discussion is a mode of learning and may not consider what their classmates say to be of any value. Unlike American students who should realize the material presented in discussion between students and teacher may be as important as the material presented in lecture format, many international students tend to ignore anything that is said by other students and therefore may miss information and opportunities for learning. One common complaint of such international students, which may appear on teacher evaluations, is that they wish the other students would be quiet so the teacher can talk.

IMPACT OF EDUCATIONAL DIFFERENCES

Because of the differences in educational systems discussed above, many international students have great difficulty in adjusting to the American system of postsecondary education. In fact, it has been posited that those international students who were most successful in the educational systems of their home countries, particularly those who did their undergraduate studies in their home countries, may have the most difficulty adapting to this new system. They have been successful in their home countries because they were able to use the learning strategies appropriate to that educational system, usually with great facility, and will continue to attempt to use those same strategies in this system, despite attempts through orientation programs to acquaint them with the differences in this system and the strategies needed for success which result from those differences.

Whether because of lack of knowledge of the differences or failure to accept and/or be able to employ new strategies for learning, students who have heretofore been considered outstanding may find that for the first time they are not among the top-level students in their classes. This realization may have a debilitating, even deleterious, effect not only on their academic performance but also on their general ability to cope with being in a different culture. Such students may present symptoms of depression, anxiety, or paranoia because they are experiencing a sort of Alice-in-Wonderland effect, i.e., the forms and formats of the educational situation are familiar enough that they think they should be able to be successful, based on previous experience, yet there is enough difference that they cannot use the same strategies and techniques which have served them well in the past and be successful in this system. They often do not realize the root of the problem lies in their expectations for student and teacher behaviors which are not met or are misinterpreted. They may experience a second level of culture shock (see Chapter 6).

Even if students are aware of the differences discussed above, they may not be able to change either their own behavior or their reaction to the behavior of American students. For example, they may know that it is accepted for American students to question what teachers say but, based on past experience in a system in which students never asked questions, they may feel uncomfortable when it happens in their classes. They still may interpret it as an inappropriate challenge to the inherent authority of the teacher. As one Taiwanese student said, "My stomach hurts after that class because the students are so rude, interrupting the teacher to ask all those questions."

Student affairs personnel often find that international students are experiencing difficulties that have roots in academic problems which have resulted from these differences. They should both be aware that such differences exist and provide the needed orientation to American educational systems which could help prevent students from finding themselves in such situations (see Chapter 6).

THE IMPACT OF CULTURAL DIFFERENCES ON ETHICAL ISSUES

The varying educational philosophies found in different cultures raise important ethical issues. One example is the general area of what is considered cheating in the American system. International students may find themselves accused of cheating because they have utilized learning strategies and behaviors which were allowed in their culture but are not accepted in this culture. One example of this was discussed earlier — the idea of copying material from a printed source verbatim. If the student's first culture held written material "sacred," then the student would be expected in that culture to reproduce what was printed, often from memory, and unchanged without any references. In the U.S. system, of course, such a performance would be plagiarism, the most heinous of academic crimes. Another example is the collaboration on homework assignments or even on tests that would be expected from students in which collaborative/cooperative learning is prized. Again, this may be seen as cheating in U.S. culture.

This requires student affairs personnel and the institution to look carefully at the institution's "judicial system." Can the same processes and punishments be applied to international students that are applied to American students? Is it possible that the international student who has indulged in behavior which in the first culture was considered appropriate should be given a probationary period before the full penalties of the judicial system are applied? For example, should a system be designed and implemented which requires international students accused of plagiarism to undergo a short course in the appropriate use of citations in U.S. academic prose and, upon successful completion of such a course, not be charged with plagiarism for that occurrence? Such a system has worked well in English as a second language classes. Students who submit papers without the proper citations are given an "F" for that assignment because the course includes instruction on citing and bibliography. They are then assigned to write a comparison/contrast paper explaining the different attitudes toward printed material in their culture versus U.S. culture, using appropriate citations. The grade for the alternate assignment then replaces the failing grade. If a similar system is adopted, it must be clearly understood by all involved that any further occurrence will be treated in the same way it would if an American student were involved.

Any modification of an institution's judicial system should be approached carefully and thoughtfully. International students should not be given special privileges simply because they are from other countries. But an informed evaluation of the possible reasons behind certain behaviors may indicate that some modifications are beneficial to both the student and the institution.

In the case of possible plagiarism, an additional important modification might be made in the orientation system, providing international students with an introduction to the appropriate use of written material as a subject that might not be part of the orientation for American students. However, many American students could benefit from some such orientation. The difference may be in its timing (in orientation classes before school begins for international students) and location (e.g., in Freshman English classes for American undergraduates). In this example, the modification to the existing system, because it occurs early in the international student's experience in the institution, might negate the need for modifying the judicial system. Another approach is to include the cultural orientation in English classes which international students are required to take (Hughes, 1984; Bagnole, 1976). But each institution must decide on its own policies, based on its available resources.

In the same way, student counseling services within an institution may need to be modified. In many cultures, it is considered inappropriate for a person to discuss personal problems with someone outside the family, which is usually defined as the extended family. Thus, students may be reluctant to make even an initial contact with the counseling office, let alone reveal to a stranger the problems they are experiencing. So counseling centers may find that they have few if any international students seeking help. The counseling center may need to modify its delivery systems and approaches to working with international students.

Counselors who have international students as potential clients need cross-cultural communication and cultural awareness if they are to be effective. Sources of information available to counselors may be faculty who teach cross-cultural communication, the foreign student adviser's office, or the international programs office (see Chapter 8).

THE SPECIAL PROBLEMS OF TEACHING ASSISTANTS

Several states have introduced laws requiring all nonnative speakers of English (usually intended to mean international students) be tested and, in some cases, trained before they are allowed to teach. Such legislation recognizes, at least tacitly, that there are expectations for teachers which are different from those for students. And this is certainly true. For example, the admissions requirements for English proficiency for international students are not in themselves adequate to screen those same students as they become teaching assistants (TAs). Just as the level of language proficiency needed by FTAs is higher, so is the necessity for their thorough understanding of the American postsecondary educational system, its philosophy and purposes, and especially the behaviors expected of students and teachers. For example, teaching assistants must not only understand the point at which cooperative learning becomes inappropriate in the U.S. system, they must recognize when such learning strategies have passed the point of being acceptable and must know how the institution's judicial system handles such situations. A physics lab instructor from Italy had difficulty recognizing whether the lab reports he received were appropriately written. He could accept the students working together during the lab, but had problems understanding that they were to write their own reports. When another lab instructor read those lab reports, those students who had done well in the Italian TA's lab section were accused of cheating — causing great problems for both the Italian lab instructor and the American students. The students had been misled into thinking that submitting the same lab report by each member of the group was an acceptable practice when, in fact, that behavior was unacceptable by the physics department and the institution.

FTAs are under even greater pressures than other international students. As students, they can continue to rely to some extent on the old ways, the ways which made them successful students in their home countries, e.g., using the reading skills that involve primarily memorizing if they are willing to spend sometimes inordinate amounts of time doing that. They can, and often do, also isolate themselves from contact with Americans and thus avoid, minimize, or mask problems caused by marginal English skills. But as teaching assistants, they cannot hide. They must be able to function in ways deemed appropriate in this culture's postsecondary educational system.

Many schools now realize the importance of special programs for FTAs. While these programs properly contain language proficiency testing and training, they must go beyond simply ensuring Level 4 English proficiency (Constantinides, 1987). They must include four other categories of information (Constantinides, forthcoming):

■ General information about U.S. educators. This includes the philosophy and purpose of education in this country and the expected behaviors of teachers and students.

■ Specific information about the institution in which the FTAs will teach. Each institution has its own "culture" which the FTAs need to understand. Types of information which should be included in this category are the demographics of the student body, admissions policies and requirements for undergraduates, traditions (e.g., using only "bluebooks" for exams or not giving tests on the day before or after a vacation), and specific teacher/student behavioral expectations (e.g., calling instructors and students by their first names or using titles).

■ Discipline-specific information. FTAs need to be made aware of the preferred teaching style of the discipline in which they will teach. This becomes especially important in those situations in which the FTAs may be students in one discipline, e.g., engineering, but teach in another, e.g., mathematics (Byrd & Constantinides, 1988).

■ Department-specific information. This topic should include such items as departmental traditions (the faculty-student softball game, which all are expected to attend even if they do not play), how graduate students are expected to address faculty, and the definition of the teaching task to which the FTA will be assigned (Byrd, 1986).

The "foreign TA problem" is one which will continue to challenge the academic community. Student affairs personnel will be involved in that challenge in a variety of ways. Thus, it is important for them to know what the requirements are in their institutions, what resources are available to potential FTAs, and how to recognize and deal with both the problems experienced by the FTAs, who may find the double burden of being a student and a teacher in an unfamiliar educational culture more than they can handle, and by the FTAs' American students. Few resources are yet available which focus on orientation for the American student who will interact with foreign teaching assistants. vom Saal (1987) and Smith (1988) have done the most interesting work to date.

CONCLUSION

Understanding the differences in educational systems and the resultant differences in the expected behaviors of students and teachers should help university administrators, faculty, and student affairs personnel deal more effectively with international students. The pressures for international students created by inadequate language skills, inappropriate study skills, or ineffective coping strategies for being a student or teacher reveal themselves in many areas of students' lives. Institutions that admit international students have a responsibility to sensitize all their personnel to the causes and effects of these pressures so they may more effectively assist them (Jenkins, 1983).

References

Althen, G. (Ed.). (1981). *Learning across cultures: Intercultural communication and international education exchange.* ERIC Document Reproduction Service No. 208 790.

Bagnole, J.W. (1976). *TEFL, perceptions, and the Arab world.* Washington, D.C.: American Friends of the Middle East.

Byrd, P. (1986). Academic subcultures within U.S. higher education: Implications for FTA training of differences in teaching styles and methods. Paper presented at the Wyoming/NAFSA Institute on Foreign TA Training.

Byrd, P., and Constantinides, J.C. (1988). FTA training programs: Searching for appropriate teaching styles. *English for Specific Purposes*, 7(2), 123-29.

Constantinides, J.C. (1987). Designing a training program for international teaching assistants. In N. Chism (Ed.), *Employment and education of teaching assistants: Readings from a national conference* (pp. 275-83). Columbus, Ohio: Center for Teaching Excellence, Ohio State University.

Constantinides, J.C. (forthcoming). Models for FTA-training programs: Focus on content.

Fieg, J., and Blair, J. (1975). *There is a difference: 12 intercultural perspectives.* Washington, D.C.: Meridian House International.

Henry, J. (1976). A cross-cultural outline of education. In J.I. Roberts and S.K. Kinsanya (Eds.), *Educational patterns and cultural configurations: The anthropology of education.* New York: David McKay Company, Inc.

Hughes, G.H. (1984). An argument for culture analysis in the second language classroom. *The American Language Journal,* 31-51.

Jenkins, H.M. (Ed.). (1983). *Educating students from other nations.* San Francisco: Jossey-Bass Publisher, Inc.

Patai, R. (1983). *The Arab mind.* New York: Charles Scribner's Sons.

Parker, O. (1976). *Cultural clues to the Middle Eastern student.* Washington, D.C.: AMIDEAST.

Saville-Troike, M. (1976). *Foundations for teaching English as a second language: Theory and method for multicultural education.* Englewood Cliffs, N.J.: Prentice-Hall.

Smith, R. (1988). You and the international TA: Paths to better understanding. Videotape. Washington, D.C.: National Association for Foreign Student Affairs.

vom Saal, D. (1987). The undergraduate experience and international teaching assistants. In N. Chism, (Ed.), *Employment and education of teaching assistants: Readings from a national conference* (pp. 167-74). Columbus, Ohio: Center for Teaching Excellence, Ohio State University.

CHAPTER TWO

Health Care for International Students

Murray M. DeArmond, M.D.
Jillian Hills Stevenson

The internationalization of higher education in the United States is now well underway. The health implications of this phenomenon must be thoughtfully addressed. It cannot be assumed that because the United States spends more dollars per capita on medical care than any other country in the world and maintains many impressive campus health programs for students that, therefore, the health needs of international students are being adequately addressed.

Health issues are sufficiently different for international students and subtleties are adequately complex to warrant special attention. With international students on some major campuses comprising over 10 percent of the total enrollment, by sheer numbers alone, this special population makes college health centers among the most challenging settings for international health work in the United States. The impact on culture is more intensified at the entry level for health care than in the referral centers of hospitals and specialized clinics in the broader community. As such, college health care staff and international student advisers must consider health care for international students from a fresh and focused perspective.

Physicians and nurses, trained in the United States, have been well schooled in clinical assessment and diagnostic procedures mostly centered on the health concerns of our culture. In training, young health care professionals are exposed to the most sophisticated technical treatment interventions available anywhere. Professional schools continue to heavily emphasize specialty activity with biomedical interests overshadowing consideration for social and psychological aspects of health. Prevention is often treated as a lower priority than treatment; therefore, many of the most inviting opportunities to address health care needs of international students may be overlooked.

From earliest recorded times, health has been viewed as the active interplay of mind, body, and spirit. This concept has special applicability for international students in its insistence on broad-based considerations and approaches to health care which are integrative in nature. From the outset, international student health issues must be considered part of a larger social phenomenon, not a dysfunction of an organ or organ system. Emotional and social aspects of health can never be set aside for later consideration. Rather, they must be addressed as central elements in health and illness patterns. The issues, themselves, extend beyond any single professional boundary. As such, a collaborative relationship should exist between student health care staff and international student advisers to plan health care for international students. Important elements of the relationship include:

° the relationship between cultural transition and stress
° medical care costs in the United States as a potential barrier to health care access

° tailored orientation programs to meet adjustment needs
° language and cultural influences
° mental health services
° prevention and education programs
° use of peers
° data collection and analysis
° nutrition.

In sum, health care services for international students simply cannot be limited to the symptoms of illness, but must relate to the well-being of individual students.

Cultural Transition

The international educational experience focuses on dislocation and transition — called by some as the "uprooting syndrome" (Gunn & Zwingmann, 1983). It represents a period of social adaptation and change from which many of the special health problems of international students arise. Only by understanding the influence of major life change on health can professionals begin to fully grasp and address the health care needs of this special population.

The homeostatic or balance theory suggests that everyone seeks a "steady state." Whenever someone is confronted with changes for which accustomed responses fail, disequilibrium ensues. This is a time of stress and exaggerated vulnerability to external influences. It is as if the steadying rudder in life has been lost, giving way to a time of uncertainty about identity and direction ahead. It is true whether one begins a new job, loses a loved one, is fired from a job, or undertakes study in a new land. Health care workers on all campuses must understand that transition impacts health. Skills and interventions responsive to this understanding will assure a successful and healthful adaptation.

The components of so-called culture shock are well known. After an initial phase of excitement and heightened awareness of the new experience, a period of adjustment characterized by an increased sense of difference follows. This can be a painful time of sadness and alienation, one of longing for familiar surroundings and loved ones. This phase can intensify to the point of temporary disengagement or complete withdrawal. For a few, in its severest form, the burdens of suicidal pressure and psychotic disorganization can occur.

For most students, given time, a period of integration and adaptation follows wherein, without giving up the importance of the earlier experience, one successfully bridges the gap into the new culture. Throughout the period of transition, students are vulnerable to illnesses which may be predominately physical or so-called psychosomatic — a combination of emotional and physical elements.

Because psychological services in many countries around the world are not well developed and often not widely accepted, students may have difficulty in comfortably getting help for the anxiety, loneliness, and depression which may be part of the transition experience. Many times these feelings are "somatized," i.e., they convert into physical symptoms. Tension headaches, fatigue, and stomachache are frequent examples. Further, changes in nutritional patterns can lead to a state of inadequate nourishment by reducing defenses against illness, predisposing students to ill health. In every dimension — physical, psychological, and social — problems can arise during the period of cultural transition as one negotiates a path from the familiar into the unfamiliar. Particularly during the first six to 10 months, the time of international education is fraught with health risks. Proper planning for health care services requires an appreciation of this frame of reference.

Traditional Western views of illness as expressions of symptoms are clearly inadequate when applied to international students. Inherent in the experience of health and illness are all the personal elements which derive from family patterns, belief systems, local traditions, personal expectations, cultural themes and interpretations, ritual practices, and nuances of language. For each person, all these elements come together in a relatively stable coherence which may be affected by any disruptive experience. It should be no wonder that Ebbin and Blankenship (1985) found that international students use campus health care services at a rate greater than their American counterparts; thereby presenting situations which are heavily weighted by psychosomatic problems.

During the uprooting and adjustment or rerooting process, several services can ameliorate stresses and protect international students' health. These services include providing adequate medical and psychological services on campus, or arranged for in the larger community, to respond to students with identified needs. Equally important is a variety of preventive measures designed to moderate the discontinuity for all students. These include programs for early case finding and education which emphasize how to maintain individual health practices for wellness. A broad-based campus program of health care for international students needs to reflect the full spectrum of responsibility from prevention to treatment. Well-developed health care programs can substantially reduce the mismatches of attitude, expectation, and information which increase the vulnerability of students to stress-related problems.

The change inherent in international study includes individual adjustment and environmental discontinuity. Well-being is predicated on harmony and balance; and, therefore, it is little wonder that during times of major change health is placed at risk. The stakes are high. In the absence of health, all else is jeopardized. Without good health, learning is threatened and academic progress can be thwarted.

Medical Costs

Most international students come to this country from homelands where costs are not a barrier to health care. In their own countries, national health care programs may offer a full range of services when needed. Many international students are confused, sometimes shocked, by the financial barriers to health care which they encounter in the United States. Even with the provision of on-campus health care for registered students, concerns are regularly expressed about difficulty getting medical care for accompanying spouses and dependent children.

Campus workers and international student advisers have an initial responsibility to provide guidance about the U.S. health care system, including its costs, arranged at the beginning of the school year. All students need to realistically anticipate paying for health care. To do otherwise can jeopardize students' access to needed treatment.

To adequately protect against burdensome costs and ensure care when needed, mandatory health insurance for international students studying in the United States and their accompanying dependents is urged. The National Association for Foreign Student Affairs (NAFSA) and the American College Health Association (ACHA) stress in a joint position statement on international student health insurance: "It is critical that institutions require adequate health insurance for all students and accompanying dependents, and determine an appropriate minimal standard of coverage in order to reduce the damaging direct costs to students" (NAFSA-ACHA, 1985).

Health Orientation

In addition to addressing costs and the role of medical insurance in the United States, all international students benefit by understanding, in detail, campus health and counseling services available to them. Each service should be thoughtfully described in an organized orientation program to include the mode of access, expectations of the system, and special programs available for international students. Health care service personnel, mental health professionals, international student peer health advisers, volunteers, and international student advisers should be involved in planning and presenting these orientation programs which can help moderate the discontinuity inherent in the transition experience.

It is particularly important for staff of health and counseling services to sensitively portray themselves to students. A health orientation program, separate from the general new student orientation, is recommended. Health care clinicians and counseling service staff should participate in orientation programs, stressing the range and competence of services, emphasizing the importance of confidentiality, and highlighting a sincere interest in serving international students. Trepidation can surround the use of institutional health care services because of concern about being sent home, uncertainties about confidentiality, and being forced to interrupt academic work. As such, staff cannot assume a traditional office-based approach. Rather, they must seek ways to actively promote their services to this special population.

Orientation programs often include general information about the importance of self-care for international students. This information can include signs to be alert to and steps to take if stresses are encountered. For example, the following might be considered:

° A description of common distress symptoms that students encounter, including headache, stomachache, other gastrointestinal (G-I) difficulty, and general fatigue. It is important to emphasize that stress symptoms affect both the body and emotions. Feelings of loneliness and anxiety, difficulty concentrating, and interruption of sleep and eating patterns are frequent early warning signs of stress.

° A discussion about the importance of maintaining regular eating and sleeping patterns. Maintaining regularity of daily activities can have a useful stabilizing influence during times of change.

° The importance of exercise. If the student has been physically active at home and comes to the United States to a relatively sedentary academic life, the experience of disjunction can be intensified. It is important for students to maintain a reasonably active lifestyle to support good health.

° A discussion about the helpfulness of breaking large problems into smaller, manageable pieces and approaching one task at a time, to completion. Such an approach is a useful strategy for those students who feel overwhelmed and paralyzed in the face of numerous obligations.

° The importance of discussing difficulties with a trusted person. For all persons, there is powerful healing tonic which comes from discussions with friends, international student advisers, health care service personnel, counselors, and others. Sharing difficulties helps alleviate burdensome stresses which may feel beyond control.

° The importance of assuring proper nutrition. A description of the role nutrition plays in overall health and a discussion of campus and community resources to ensure a well-balanced diet can be helpful.

° Urging students to identify the circumstances and location where they feel most relaxed and comfortable. This might be in the library (alone or with friends) or joining others at the student union, at a friend's apartment, or in one's residence hall. Having identified the source of comfort, it is important to spend at least one-half hour, three times a week, in that situation to relax from the stresses encountered. This simple tactic can help restore needed balance during a difficult adjustment to a new culture.

Other programs to increase international students' awareness of health care have included open houses, small group discussions between health care professionals and international students at the student health center, and the use of specified staff, introduced to international students as "contact personnel" who will be available to international students in need.

Because students' spouses and children often are not eligible for campus health care services, health and mental health staff should identify adequate health care for them. This may require meeting with community-based health care professionals to develop agreements to assist family members in getting health care needs met. As with international students, special orientation programs for dependents have been helpful by providing information and responding to families' concerns about health care in the United States. Such orientation programs might include:

° available campus or community resources
° appropriate use of emergency services
° information on health care choices (public or private, preventive, holistic, homeopathic, self-care)
° information on health care professionals (specialists, dentists, physical therapists, optometrists)
° health insurance
° support for language difficulties
° personal safety
° cultural customs and health

Health orientation programs may be initiated and coordinated by the international student services office but, again, require the active involvement of the campus health and mental health services staff.

Language, Culture, and Health

Language can create an early barrier to health care. A campus team including international student advisers, student health care service personnel, and counseling staff will want to make available a variety of written materials translated to serve the linguistic needs of the major groups represented in the international student population. In addition, many campuses have provided interpreter lists, providing names of interested volunteers on and off campus willing to help bridge language barriers for students. Faculty and staff with international backgrounds, foreign students, and interested community members comprise a powerful resource of individuals who share some cultural background with prospective student patients. Such individuals can be of enormous help in providing needed communication and support at a level of sophistication and nuance often required when dealing with issues as personal as those of health and illness.

In addition to language, a student's background, accustomed patterns of care at home, and health belief systems may make the Western medical system and its institutional nature seem alien. To reduce the mismatches of cultural expectation and discomfort, campus health care professionals are encouraged to participate in continuing in-service education to increase their awareness and sensitivity to the special needs of international students. Presentations on special health needs of women from different cultures, updates on "exotic" diseases which may be encountered, and reviews of special health risks of international students have been found to be quite helpful. Programs on hepatitis B and malaria, for example, might be covered. Panel discussions by international students, including descriptions of health care in their home countries and inviting their comments about experience in this country, should be a part of staff training for health care and mental health professionals. These educational programs can be supplemented by texts on tropical medicine and references on infectious diseases not commonly seen among American students to help assure proper staff support. A comprehensive program to enhance staff skills can bridge cultural gaps which delay or impede the provision of health care on campus.

No one program for staff, no matter how well intentioned, can hope to encompass all the information and sensitivity needed to address cultural differences worldwide. However, the campus is a rich community from which to draw. The variety of faculty, staff, and student backgrounds mentioned earlier provides a valuable resource to help reduce the discontinuities international students experience. As well, clinicians need to listen for and incorporate cultural beliefs into the clinical setting. It is important to raise questions about how the student would/might handle a similar situation at home. How might the family respond? What might be the personal meaning of a particular illness or disease? These inquiries can be extremely helpful in bringing a clinician's focus on symptoms and disease together with a student's illness.

Mental Health

A special set of circumstances surrounds mental health care. Many international students, not unlike American students, find it difficult to face the need for mental health counseling. Too often, availing oneself of mental health care may be feared as revealing inadequacy or viewed as a shameful act. And yet, many health problems faced by international students are stress related, a natural consequence of the changes experienced in cross-cultural education. Because the health care needs of international students are frequently complex interactions of the mind and body, no single discipline or one professional response is adequate. Again, international student advisers, health care professionals, and psychological staff working together are needed to best meet the needs of students.

A student being seen by a physician in the general medical clinic may benefit by the invitation of a mental health staff member to join a discussion on the relationship between medical symptoms and psychological distress. It is important for all campus staff to listen both for the symptoms (biomedical experience) and the personal reaction (i.e., psychological experience) the student is encountering. Sometimes an educational offering is a helpful first step. Giving a student a clear explanation of the relationship between body symptoms and the world of feelings and emotions can provide a useful frame of reference from which a student can draw strength and which may make a mental health referral more acceptable. A referral which may be effective for American students by simply giving them an appointment at a distant clinic across campus is often ineffective for international students. A thorough discussion and supplemental written instructions are often helpful in gaining student understanding and subsequent compliance.

In summary, in working with international students, mental health professionals will want to

° Listen carefully to the student's experience to make a connection between the student's views and those of the counselor
° Use the language of the body and medicine, which may be more familiar to the student, to explain related emotional experiences which the student may be encountering
° Be flexible in the approach to international students. There is nothing sacred about the length of a counseling session.

Sometimes a series of brief 15- to 20-minute sessions arranged outside the clinical office setting should be considered. Including friends the student may want to bring along to therapy sessions can be useful.
° Consider an active, directive approach. By temporarily taking over some decision making for a student, the therapist can lend a patient needed ego strength during a temporary period until the student can build sufficient internal strength. As on other occasions, a written plan of care can be helpful.

Prevention
The general medical care system in the United States has focused on treatment in hospitals. Physicians and other health care professionals are trained in diagnosis and treatment; training in prevention and education are encountered only peripherally in the curriculum. Therefore, there is an unfortunate tendency to downplay individual responsibility for health and generations of patients have become dependent on the health care system to meet their needs.

One of the highlights of campus health care programs in the United States has been the development of some of the most innovative prevention and education programs to be found anywhere. These have grown in response to the inviting opportunities of working with students, ever eager to learn about their lives and the relationship between behavior and health, and to the influence of educational institutions of which they are a part. College health care services seek to develop programs in primary prevention (education for all students) and secondary prevention (identifying at-risk students for early intervention). An appropriate balance of treatment and prevention services is sought to best meet students' needs. For international students, campus health programs for smoking cessation, drug and alcohol education, sexually transmitted diseases (STD) prevention, HIV infection/AIDS education, and stress management can be among the most helpful health resources both during a transition period and later.

Peer Support for Health

To assure effective, complete health care services, international students should be encouraged to participate in the campus health care system. Including international students on student health advisory committees and encouraging them to serve as peer health advocates can support this effort. International students can assist with the evaluation of health programs and services and insurance programs, participate in developing health service budgets, review policy development, and plan new services.

Successful health education programs have included the use of trained peer health advocates to relay sensitive health information on topics such as AIDS and other STDs, dating customs in the United States, and birth control, as well as information on general health topics. Some peer health advocate programs offer credit to the volunteers, while others offer incentive gifts such as discount bookstore coupons. NAFSA maintains a list of peer health advocate programs through its national clearinghouse on international student health resources.

Data

It is crucial to maintain and analyze health data on international students. Very little has been written on health needs of this special population, and each campus has an obligation to compile aggregate information to better understand needs and to plan programs. We need to know the students to better understand the kinds of health problems occurring, to be knowledgeable about the demographics of the students served, and to regularly assess needs and interests of international students. The data base becomes necessary for quality assurance activities. Only through information can problems be identified and practices be audited against performance standards. Consistent data collection and peer review can help strengthen the ability to provide culturally sensitive, effective health care programs.

Nutrition

Nutrition is a major area of concern among many international students. Meal time is an experience which nourishes the human spirit in the company of family and friends, in addition to strengthening the body from the food consumed. Students coming to the United States may be unprepared to shop in a setting where some foods may be unfamiliar and packaged in unrecognizable ways. They may be unaware of a variety of local restaurants which might have dishes familiar to them.

Some international students have fallen into the habit of limiting themselves to a narrow base of fast foods or a few prepackaged items only to find these present a long-term threat to their well-being. Campus officials, including staff of the international student services office, can help address these needs through programs of accompanied trips to nearby supermarkets to discuss the kind of foods which are available, explaining differences. On some campuses, special cookbooks, cooking classes, and orientation to nearby ethnic restaurants have been helpful to international students in their adaptation to the United States.

NATIONAL ACTIVITIES

The National Association for Foreign Student Affairs (NAFSA) and the American College Health Association (ACHA) have, through the years, addressed the special health care concerns of international students and their dependents. In 1986, the NAFSA/ACHA Joint Task Force on Foreign Student Health Care was formed to improve the delivery of culturally appropriate health care to international students. Two years later, the task force, serving as a model of interassociational cooperation, was approved as a committee by the Boards of Directors of NAFSA and ACHA.

The committee has sponsored several innovative projects to assist health care providers and international student advisers address the special health care needs of international students. These projects include a NAFSA/ACHA Joint Position Statement on Foreign Student Health Insurance; a program of national health workshops that brings together international student advisers and health care providers to improve communication/collaboration; a national computer-based clearinghouse on international student health information and resources, HealthLink; and a publication entitled *Optimizing Health Care for Foreign Students in the U.S. and American Students Abroad* (NAFSA-ACHA, 1989). Future activities include publishing an international health newsletter, *Optimizing Health: International Connections*; a compilation of briefs on the health systems of various countries; and a continuation of the national health workshops.

Focusing the efforts of both associations to the special health care needs of international students and dependents has been vital to the committee's success. As emphasized throughout this chapter, the collaboration and cooperation of international student advisers and student health care staff is an important key to improving health care for international students and their dependents.

CONCLUSION

Health care for international students calls for activities on many levels — from institution-wide programs to those involving individual contact. Both prevention and treatment services should be provided. Multiple offices and disciplines must collaborate; international students should be actively involved in all facets of program development. The challenge for campus staff to understand the special health needs of international students is great. Making connections among various cultural and social traditions is a key concept to help students with health needs.

At the institutional level, it is most important for leaders of colleges and universities to expressly assert the value of international students on campus. The presence of international students enhances the richness of the educational experience for all. International students need to understand how highly valued they are as part of higher education for all students. That sincere expression of support can help create a climate which fosters healthy adaptation among all students.

References

Ebbin, A., and Blankenship, E. (1985). *A national survey of college health centers on health care for international students.* Washington, D.C.: National Association for Foreign Student Affairs.

Gunn, A., and Zwingmann, C. (1983). *Uprooting and health: Psycho-social problems of students from abroad.* Albany, N.Y.: World Health Organization.

National Association for Foreign Student Affairs (NAFSA)-American College Health Association (ACHA). (1985). *Position statement: Health insurance for foreign* students. Washington, D.C.: National Association for Foreign Student Affairs.

National Association for Foreign Student Affairs (NAFSA)-American College Health Association (ACHA). (1989). *Optimizing health care for foreign students in the United States and American students abroad.* Washington, D.C.: National Association for Foreign Student Affairs.

CHAPTER THREE

Legal Issues Affecting International Students

Peter S. Levitov

Student affairs professionals are faced with a burgeoning number of legal concerns in their daily work. Because they provide services to international students, the scope of these concerns is significantly broadened. Some areas of responsibility in student affairs (e.g., campus activities, recreation) are affected by the presence of international students on campus only to a slight degree. Other student affairs areas (e.g., placement, housing) are affected more so. Admissions requires a staff member with both specialized training and a set of printed resources to perform within the basic legal framework established for institutions authorized to enroll international students. Advising and counseling are so affected by the legal issues unique to international students that they virtually require the designation of one or more professionals to administer a range of specialized services and programs for this population.

Presented here is a skeletal summary of the U.S. immigration laws (Immigration and Nationality Act, 1952) and regulations (Aliens and Nationality, Foreign Relations, Title 8, 22 Code of Federal Regulations, 1990) regarding international students. It serves two purposes: first, to portray the legal setting in which international students matriculate at our colleges and universities; and second, to highlight the legal parameters which govern student affairs professionals in their work with international students. This chapter also identifies several key legal issues for student affairs staff, providing contextual examples in which several of these issues may and do arise.

Because about 80 percent of the more than 400,000 international students in the United States hold the F-1 (student) visa classification (Zikopoulos, 1991), this chapter focuses on the legal issues affecting them. Should the issues differ significantly according to visa classification, the discussion will note these differences.

IMMIGRATION-RELATED CONCERNS

Before an educational institution may enroll international students in the F-1 visa classification, it must apply for approval from the U.S. Immigration and Naturalization Service (INS). The application process includes designating up to five school officials who certify that they have read, understand, and will follow federal regulations pertaining to international students. Violating these regulations may result in the loss of their institution's approval to enroll F-1 students. This is not a perfunctory certification by any means. It involves a complex aggregation of regulations that have befuddled senior international student administrators and immigration attorneys — not to mention the INS itself.

Institutions seeking to sponsor an exchange visitor program for participants in the J-1 visa classification must seek approval from the U.S. Information Agency. Such sponsorship may encompass exchange faculty, visiting scholars, and other participants in educational interchange, as well as students.

Admission
The INS has established regulations of institutional responsibility for enrolling F-1 students. Whereas institutions establish their own criteria for enrolling domestic students, INS regulations mandate that international students be not only academically admissible, but also proficient in the English language to the extent necessary for full-time study at the institution and be financially capable of meeting the tuition, fees, and living expenses estimated for full-time attendance. These criteria must be met for both international students (F-1) and exchange visitor students (J-1). Upon matriculation, international students receive Form I-20 AB and exchange students receive Form IAP-66.

Recruitment activities are directly affected by INS regulations. Higher education institutions must evaluate a written application plus academic records, language proficiency assessments, and financial documentation, at the institution's location in the United States, before Form I-20 AB can be issued. In other words, an admissions officer may not offer admission to an international student while on a recruiting trip, whether to Jakarta or to Jersey City. Furthermore, no fee can be charged for the form.

While approval to enroll international students need not be sought periodically, as with accreditation, institutions must notify the INS when major curricular changes and changes in academic programs with employment components occur. They must also submit certifications by newly designated school officials of their intention to follow the pertinent regulations.

International students seeking to travel to the United States, with few exceptions not relevant to this discussion, must obtain a passport from their country of citizenship. With Form I-20 AB and passport in hand, along with documentation of finances, they must apply for a visa to enter the United States at one of the U.S. embassies or consulates around the world. If granted, the visa will be stamped on a page in their passport and they may travel to the United States. If their documentation is in order and the INS inspector at the port of entry is convinced that they are not intending to immigrate to the United States, a requirement inherent in all nonimmigrant visa classifications, the students will be permitted to enter the country in the F-1 visa classification. The particulars of their admission will be stamped in their passports and they will be given two documents: the second sheet (pages 3-4) of Form I-20 AB and INS Form I-94, Departure Record, recording the entry, date, port, visa classification, and date to which their stay in the United States is valid. This date is usually noted as "Duration of Status (D/S)," meaning as long as the student is maintaining lawful status in the educational program designated on Form I-20 AB.

Admissions officers must not encourage students with partially completed admission dossiers to travel to the United States as tourists (with the B-2 visa) and assume they will be able to change to the F-1 classification after admission. The INS will deny an application to change nonimmigrant classification from B-2 to F-1 because the student will be deemed to have misrepresented their true intentions to the U.S. Consul and the INS inspector.

There are, however, a few ways in which intending students can come to this country before being fully accepted by a college or university. Students may apply for a B-2 visa with the special notation "prospective student" if

° the student has not yet selected a school and comes to the United States to visit more than one school
° the student with Form I-20 AB intends to enter the United States more than 90 days before the initial semester begins
° the student has evidence of admission but no Form I-20 AB
° the student needs to take an exam or have an interview before admission is granted (Immigration and Naturalization Student/Schools Operations Instructions, 248.7 [d], 1985).

If students without a B-2 "prospective student" notation do enter, subsequently receive Form I-20 AB and are denied a change to F-1 classification, they must leave the United States and apply for the F-1 visa at a U.S. embassy or consulate abroad. Admissions officers, therefore, should not encourage intending students to travel until admission is formalized, a Certificate of Eligibility (Form I-20 AB or Form IAP-66) is received, and they have a student or exchange visitor visa.

Higher education institutions must keep documentation on which the admission decision is made and the Certificate of Eligibility is issued for one year beyond the date on which admitted students are no longer enrolled at the institution. Students already in the United States in other visa classifications need to apply to the INS for change of nonimmigrant classification but may enroll before receiving approval of the change.

Full-time students on the F-1 visa who wish to transfer must notify the INS by informing their previous school of their intention to transfer and then reporting to the official at the new institution named on Form I-20 AB within 15 days of the beginning of classes of the new semester. The designated school official at the new school should finalize the transfer within 30 days of the beginning of classes and mark the student's Form I-20 AB, page 4, in accordance with the regulations. The designated school official should also photocopy the form after making notations, if any, for the student's files to comply with record-keeping responsibilities. Students who attend one institution, leave the United States, and return to enroll at another institution accomplish the transfer simply by presenting Form I-20 AB issued by the new institution at the port of entry.

There are also regulations for notifying the INS that F-1 students are undertaking a new educational program (meaning a new degree level rather than a new major) at the same institution. This procedure is somewhat comparable to the transfer notification procedure.

Maintenance of Status
To maintain legal status, international students must attend the school authorized on Form I-20 AB submitted either to an INS inspector at the port of entry or to a designated school official at the institution to which the students are transferring. Students may not initially enter the United States on Form I-20 AB issued by one institution and enroll in another institution unless they have either attended the authorized school for at least one semester or have first reported in person to the authorized school and begun the matriculation process. Students must pursue a full course of study, defined as a minimum of 12 hours for undergraduate students and that which an institution deems full time for graduate students. Exceptions exist for documented medical reasons and for certain academic reasons such as needing less than full-time enrollment in the final semester to complete an educational program. Regulations prescribe particular enrollment criteria for intensive English language programs and other types of educational institutions.

As noted earlier, Form I-20 AB indicates the expected date of completion for the students' educational programs. This date is based upon a reasonable estimate by a designated school official of the time an average international student would need to complete a similar program in that discipline. A grace period of no more than one year may be added to and included in the estimate. Students needing more time than the period indicated may be granted an extension by their institution for compelling academic or medical reasons. If an extension is granted, the institution must notify the INS of the new completion date. At the conclusion of their educational programs, which may include a period of authorized employment for practical training, international students have 60 days in which to depart the country or apply for another visa classification to remain in the United States.

All aliens, including students, must report any change of U.S. address to the INS, usually by mailing a postcard, within ten days of the change. Students who violate their status may, in some instances, apply to the INS for reinstatement. Reinstatement is not available, however, to students who engage in unauthorized employment.

Employment
International students who are "in status" may be employed on campus by an institution they are authorized to attend or on campus by a commercial establishment that serves students, such as a bookstore or catering service, but not, for example, by a building contractor engaged in construction on campus. On-campus employment which is an integral part of students' educational programs also may be performed off campus as long as the employment is formally associated with the school's curriculum or is related to contractually funded research at the graduate level. This employment is limited to 20 hours per week

while school is in session, but is not limited during school vacation periods.

Students who are in good standing at the institution, however, may not be "in status" with regard to immigration regulations and, consequently, may not be eligible for on-campus employment. Failure to pursue a full course of study and failure to process a transfer within the time limits established by regulation are two examples of violations of status that render F-1 students ineligible for part-time employment on campus. Furthermore, international students may not displace a domestic worker, although there is no rule precluding the replacement of a domestic worker, and they may not work during a strike or other labor dispute.

The Immigration Reform and Control Act of 1986 and attendant regulations (Aliens and Nationality, Title 8 Code of Federal Regulations Part 274a, 1990) established rigorous procedures by which employers must document the employment eligibility of all new employees. Noncompliance by an employer, either by hiring aliens not authorized to be employed or by failing to comply with the documentation requirements, may result in severe penalties.

International students must present identification (such as a passport or state-issued driver's license with photograph) and a document of employment eligibility. For F-1 students, the latter document would be pages 3-4 of Form I-20 AB issued for the students' current degree level, properly noted by the INS that they have entered the United States to attend that school, or noted by the designated school official at the new school that the INS has been notified of their transfer to that school, or that the student is continuing in another educational program at the same school.

There are extremely stringent regulations that govern off-campus employment, including internships.

Beginning October 1991 for a 3-year pilot period, F-1 students may be employed part time off campus during the academic year and without restriction in vacation periods if certain conditions are met: the students have been in the F-1 classification for 12 months; they are in good academic standing at their authorized institution; and their intended employer files an attestation that it has been unable to hire U.S. workers for at least 60 days and that it is offering wages and working conditions that are at least equal to those offered to others in similar positions at the place of employment (Immigration Act, 1990).

International students who have been enrolled in an academic program on a full-time basis for at least nine consecutive months may engage in practical training directly related to their major area of study both before and after completing their programs of study.

Curricular practical training (e.g., internship, practicum, cooperative education, alternate work-study program), which is an integral part of students' programs of study, may also be authorized by a designated school official. Curricular practical training must be either required for a degree program or it must be a credit course listed in the institution's catalog. Graduate students whose programs of study require immediate participation in curricular practical training are exempted from the nine-month, in-status requirement. Authorization is documented by a designated school official on page 4 of Form I-20 AB. Students who engage in one year or more of full-time curricular practical training are precluded from seeking postcompletion practical training.

After completing a degree or between degrees, students may engage in up to 12 months of postcompletion practical training if recommended by a designated school official and so noted on page 4 of their Form I-20 AB. Such training must be related to their major and commensurate with their educational level. International students receiving permission must travel to the INS office serving that jurisdiction and apply for an Employment Authorization Document, INS Form I 688B, a photo identification card issued for verifying employment eligibility.

Students who work on campus do not need an Employment Authorization Document because as long as they are maintaining status such employment authorization is inherent in their visa classification.

J-1 students may engage in practical training for up to 18 months after completing their programs of study. This is accomplished by letter from the ''responsible officer'' of the exchange visitor program if there is time remaining on their Form I-94. If not, the responsible officer may issue a new form IAP-66 for practical training with which the students apply to the INS for an extension of stay.

Reporting

Occasionally, each college and university must report on the status of international students authorized to attend the institution. From its data base, the INS generates Student Status Form I-721 which lists all F-1 students known to be authorized to attend that institution. Designated school officials must return the form within 60 days, coding the students as to full time, less than full time, on practical training, never attended, transferred, etc. They must also add the names of other international students to whom the institution has recently issued Form I-20 AB and are enrolled. Legal concerns raised by the process are examined later in this chapter. J-1 students no longer participating in an exchange visitor program are reported to the INS as they become disaffiliated.

VISA CLASSIFICATIONS

International students hold many types of visa classifications, in addition to the F-1 classification. The other classifications include

■ F-2: If these immediate family members attend school, they are not required to enroll in a full course of study. The institution has no immigration-related responsibilities related to their admission, record keeping, or reporting, with the exception of issuing documents in the name of the F-1 principal visa holders to enable dependents to apply for the F-2 visa to enter or re-enter the United States to join F-1 students. F-2 dependents may not be gainfully employed (on campus or elsewhere) in the United States.

■ J-1: The Exchange Visitor Program, administered by the U.S. Information Agency, enables a variety of educational and cultural visitors to utilize the J-1 visa. Although privately supported or institutionally supported international students are not prohibited from participating in exchange visitor programs, participation is generally reserved to students who are in formal exchange programs, are sponsored by a government (either the U.S. or foreign), or are sponsored by international organizations in the exchange field.

There are several parallels between F-1 students and J-1 students. Some of the salient differences are:

° J-1 students receive Form IAP-66 rather than Form I-20 AB
° J-1 students may not lawfully stay in the United States after the specified date noted on Form I-94. It is generally 30 days after the expected date of completion of their educational program indicated on Form IAP-66.
° J-1 students may only work according to the terms of a scholarship, fellowship, or assistantship. Incidental

on-campus employment is not permitted. In cases of unforeseen need, the responsible officer of the exchange visitor program may authorize part-time employment, either on or off campus.

° J-1 students may transfer (change exchange visitor program sponsor) only if the intended transfer is clearly consistent with the original or a closely related program objective as indicated on the former Form IAP-66. There are special procedures to request a change of program sponsor.

° J-1 practical training may be awarded only after completion of a degree or certificate but it may be authorized for up to 18 months.

° Many J-1 students are ineligible to change their visa classification in the United States (or obtain H-1, L-1, or permanent resident visa at a U.S. embassy or consulate abroad) until they have lived in the country of their permanent residence at least two years. Students subject to the home country residence requirement are those whose skills are in short supply in their home countries and specified on the U.S. Information Agency's Exchange Visitors Skills List, who have been financially supported by their own government or financially supported by the U.S. government in a program established for international exchange, or who have come to the United States for graduate medical training. Waivers of the two-year home country residence requirement may be obtained in very special circumstances.

■ J-2: As with F-2 dependents, J-2 dependents may attend school. The institution has similar, limited facilitative responsibilities with respect to the entry and re-entry of J-2 family members. The key difference is that they may seek permission from the INS to be employed for their own maintenance and support. If such permission is granted, a notation is made on Form I-94 and an Employment Authorization Document must be obtained. Once authorized, employment is not restricted to time or place.

■ M-1: Students admitted to vocational or technical schools or to vocational or technical programs within more comprehensive institutions are issued Form I-20 MN. Some of the critical differences between M-1 students and F-1 students are: M-1 students may not transfer to academic programs or change their nonimmigrant visa classification to F-1, M-1 students may not be employed on or off campus, and M-1 students may engage only in a more circumscribed period of practical training.

■ M-2: Regulations pertaining to dependents of M-1 students are virtually identical to those pertaining to F-2 dependents.

    The foregoing discussion will not qualify the reader as an international student adviser, no less an immigration attorney. Rather, it is intended to frame the international students and their institutions in a complex regulatory scheme which affects colleges and universities long before the students arrive on campus. Institutions and student affairs staff who understand the "big picture" of immigration issues will be able to provide services and programs to international students without compromising either the students or their institutions from a legal perspective.

OTHER CONCERNS

Confidentiality of Records/Mandatory Reporting Requirements

The Family Educational Rights and Privacy Act (1974), commonly known as the Buckley Amendment or FERPA, applies to all students. Among other things, it limits the information a higher education institution can disclose about students without their formal consent. The items which may be disclosed are collectively known as "directory information," although there are circumstances (such as information relating to an immediate danger to life or safety or information to enable a decision to be made regarding an award of financial aid) that further open the window of disclosure. Even directory information may be kept private if students so request.

Registration and records offices as well as international student advisers and academic units may be asked for information beyond that authorized by FERPA. Some inquiries such as grade reports are easily deflected, as they would be for domestic students. Other inquiries may pertain specifically to international students such as visa classification, source of financial support, and requests for lists of students from particular countries. Likewise, this information may not be disclosed, whether the request is made by an embassy official, the INS, a law enforcement agency, a parent, a bill collector, or an entrepreneur. Formal requests by the INS are discussed separately.

Frequently institutions may receive well-intentioned requests for the names of "students from Country X." Such requests usually come from the media seeking an informed response to a news item, an elementary school wanting a resource for a particular class, or from a civic association seeking luncheon speakers. It would be wise to develop a consent form by which international students may agree to be available as representatives or "cultural ambassadors" of Country X for such inquiries.

Federal regulations specify that certain records be kept and certain reports be made regarding international students. All international students, as a prerequisite to being granted the F-1 visa and being permitted to enter the United States, must sign a certification on Form I-20 AB. This statement reads in part: "I also authorize the named school to release any information from my records, which is needed by the INS pursuant to 8 CFR 214.3(g) [Title 8

Code of Federal Regulations Part 214.3 (g)] to determine my nonimmigrant status." Questions have been raised regarding whether this is a knowing waiver and, as such, permits the educational institution to make virtually limitless disclosures to the INS. Legal authorities differ on this issue.

Since the INS needs to know the status of aliens in the United States, school officials must report this information to the INS. The Student Status Form (I-721) is used for such reporting. Since students reported to be less than full time may be "written up" for deportation for having violated their F-1 status, it is important that designated school officials verify information that could be disadvantageous to international students before certifying that information on the form. Therefore, school officials are advised to contact students who are underenrolled to ascertain if they meet the INS alternative criteria for full-time status as noted earlier. Were students to be deported or otherwise be damaged (e.g., having to pay an attorney for representation in a deportation hearing) on account of faulty or negligent reporting on Form I-721, liability could be imposed on the institution. Regulations also require designated school officials to make available to the INS any of the records the institution is obligated to keep but they do not require disclosure to any agency except the INS. School officials should not release information except pursuant to these regulations. A school official should not disclose information on students' employment, marital status, lifestyles, or personal conduct.

An institution's approval to enroll international students can be withdrawn for failure to comply with the regulations. It is critical, therefore, for all staff members in admissions, registration, records, and international student advising to be familiar with the regulations and to follow them precisely. At the same time, colleges and universities need to maintain appropriate relationships with students and their families, sponsors, and governments. Release forms should be developed for such commonplace occurrences in the international student experience as reporting grades to students' embassies or sponsors. *The Adviser's Manual of Federal Regulations Affecting Foreign Students and Scholars* (Bedrosian, 1992) is an essential road map to compliance.

Counseling

In some instances, students perceive the international student adviser as an enforcer rather than an advocate, an agent of the government rather than an educator. These students may choose not to disclose to their international student adviser something that could be embarrassing or in violation of their immigration status. Consequently, other student affairs agencies such as counseling centers may become the repository for the confidences of international students. Counselors are bound by professional codes of ethics regarding confidentiality. International student advisers are likewise obligated to maintain information in strict confidence (National Association for Foreign Student Affairs, 1989). In fact, they sustain a greater burden because they may be the only institutional representatives in whom international students feel they can repose the trust necessary to make certain disclosures. Counselors, therefore, must be careful about offering advice, encouraging or endorsing students' actions that could jeopardize their status. Basic knowledge of INS regulations by college counseling staff is desirable but also quite unrealistic in most campus counseling settings. Direct contact with the international student adviser, or a helpful adviser at a nearby institution, while maintaining the confidentiality of student clients as appropriate, will educate counselors as to the legal ramifications of the range of alternatives available to the students.

Marital or family counseling presents special legal issues. While divorce may be an appropriate counseling consideration for a married couple in certain circumstances, it may not be possible for them to obtain a divorce. If the state where they reside requires the petitioning party to be a resident of that state and residency is viewed as inconsistent with nonimmigrant status in the United States, there would be no jurisdiction to entertain a legal action for divorce. Furthermore, the immigration status of dependent family members is wholly derivative of the principal visa holder. If a marriage is dissolved, the nonstudent spouse has no legal standing in the United States absent an independent visa classification.

International students may violate their status by receiving certain public benefits. For example, regulations specifically render international students ineligible for federally subsidized housing. Since all international students have certified on Form I-20 AB that they have sufficient resources to attend school in the United States, the INS considers the acceptance of certain public benefits such as Aid For Dependent Children and food stamps to be inconsistent with maintaining lawful nonimmigrant status. Consequently, nonimmigrant recipients of some public benefits may be denied important privileges under the immigration laws, such as the opportunity to change to another nonimmigrant classification or to adjust their status to permanent resident. They also may become deportable. Often social service agencies are not aware of these restrictions. Referrals, therefore, should be made with great caution and only after discussing these limitations with the students, lest international students or their family members violate status by improperly accepting a public benefit. Children born of international students in the United States, of course, are citizens of this country and are eligible for all government benefits — for themselves only.

Affirmative Action/Equal Opportunity

Affirmative action laws affect permanent hiring by federal contractors. Since international students are not eligible for permanent employment by virtue of their nonimmigrant visa status, they are beyond the scope of these rules which affect U.S. citizens and lawful permanent residents (i.e., immigrants) of the United States.

"Persons" are granted equal educational opportunities and equal employment opportunities. International students, being within this protected class, may not be deprived of equal treatment. Examples of unlawful discrimination which might arise in a student affairs context include the denial of housing in particular residence halls and the refusal of recreational space on campus. It also would be unlawful for an institution to exclude international students from consideration for student employment, provided the positions are not restricted to citizens or permanent residents (e.g., college work-study jobs) and the students are permitted by immigration regulations to accept such employment.

Health and Death Issues

As noted in the previous chapter, health care raises special issues for international students. Few institutions are affiliated with a teaching hospital and fewer still employ a staff physician specializing in tropical diseases. Nevertheless, if students continually present certain types of ailments, an institution might incur liability if it neglected to treat them, particularly if there were epidemiological ramifications. While an institution might require certain medical tests of students coming from regions known to be afflicted with particular diseases, it might be held liable for failure to take corrective action regarding students who exhibit symptoms of contagious diseases (e.g., tuberculosis) that potentially could affect other members of the campus community.

Mandatory health insurance for international students is one issue over which legal minds disagree. There has been a division of opinion as to whether an institution may require health insurance of international students if such insurance is not required of all students. An Ohio federal court in *Ahmed v. The University of Toledo* (1986) upheld an institutional insurance requirement. While the ruling is not binding on other states, it is an indication that courts may find there is no constitutional impediment to imposing this requirement.

On occasion, educational institutions are confronted with the death of an international student. Decisions regarding embalmment, burial, cremation, and the repatriation of bodily remains raise issues with serious implications in other cultures. Advice should be sought from the deceased student's national or religious groups prior to making arrangements with a mortician. The tragedy of death raises protocal issues with the student's government, privacy issues, religious issues, and issues pertaining to the student's personal property, as well as concerns with legal obligations such as apartment rent and repayment of loans. Burak (1987) offers excellent guidance in this area.

Several health and accident policies written for participants in international educational exchange have a rider covering the repatriation of remains. In light of the cost of preparing a body for shipment and transporting a coffin, institutions negotiating with insurance carriers for group coverage might include this provision and, if insurance is required, require repatriation and/or life insurance as well as health and accident insurance.

Financial Aid, Student Employment, and Taxation

Institutions may not award federal financial aid (e.g., grants, loans, college work-study employment) to nonimmigrant international students. Not only would school officials jeopardize their programs by so doing but students, by accepting such aid even if awarded erroneously, would violate their immigration status.

Although most institutions are well versed in the employer sanctions provisions of the Immigration Reform and Control Act (1986), international student employment is governed by a complex maze of regulations, as discussed earlier. Advice in this realm should be sought by financial aid advisers and placement officials from the campus international student adviser and from *The Adviser's Manual of Federal Regulations Affecting Foreign Students and Scholars* (Bedrosian, 1992).

F-1 students and J-1 students who are lawfully employed are exempt from Social Security (Employees' Benefits, Title 20 Code of Federal Regulations Part 404.1036, 1991). Neither the employer nor the employee makes a contribution. J-2 students who are lawfully employed are not so covered; consequently, contributions are withheld from J-2 employees' wages and are matched and remitted by the employer.

Federal and state income taxation for international students is quite complex. F-1 students and J-1 students who earn money in the United States are required to file a federal income tax return, Internal Revenue Service Form 1040NR. They are taxed only on U.S.-source income, including the portion of graduate assistantships that exceed a tuition waiver. The waiver is considered a scholarship and, as such, is tax exempt. Except for citizens of a very few countries, Form 1040NR provides for one personal exemption but not for exemptions for immediate family members. Furthermore, international students are not permitted the standard deduction and married students generally may not file joint returns. After five years in the F-1 classification or after 2 years in the J-1 classification, students may under certain conditions be eligible to file

Form 1040, the resident income tax return. While this permits exemptions and deductions not allowed on Form 1040NR, it subjects the students to reporting and paying on worldwide income (such as salary paid while on study leave, investment income from an overseas source).

As of this writing (April 1992), 39 countries have negotiated income tax treaties with the United States. *U.S. Tax Treaties* (U.S. Department of the Treasury, 1990) covers these treaties and their provisions. This booklet should be reviewed by an institution's payroll office to determine whether students are wholly or partially exempt from federal income tax and, if so, to prepare Forms W-4 accordingly.

Aliens leaving the United States, whether temporarily or permanently, are required to obtain a Certificate of Tax Compliance (Internal Revenue Service Form 1040 C), also known as a "sailing permit," before departure. F-1 students and J-2 dependents who have ever earned money in this country and all J-1 students, whether or not they earned money in the United States, must comply with this requirement.

State income tax laws do not follow a consistent pattern and must be examined carefully to determine the liability of international students. Many states impose tax liability based upon the federal income tax return but unique provisions distinguish one state's requirements from another's. States may also utilize formulas for taxpayers who lived only part of the year in that state.

Student Organizations

Many international students join together in organizations or associations of people with a common heritage. These groups may be identified by nationality, geographical region, religion, or even by an athletic activity (e.g., cricket) which might not otherwise take place on campus.

Students from a particular country generally form an association to provide a vehicle for individuals away from home to reinforce their ties to their country and culture through such interactions as celebration of holidays, enjoyment of food, music, films, and relaxed conversation in their first language. To open the membership of that association to students from other countries, including the United States, may seem in conflict with the very purpose of the group. Nevertheless, institutional endorsement of restricted membership provisions in the constitutions of such associations may run afoul of antidiscrimination laws in the Civil Rights Act (1964).

Religious activities on a public institution campus also raise legal concerns which, at this time, are not yet resolved. These may arise in the context of international student associations formed on the basis of religious affiliation. While the U.S. Supreme Court has recognized that an institution "has the right to exclude even First Amendment activities that violate reasonable campus rules or substantially interfere with the opportunity of other students to obtain an education" (*Widmar v. Vincent*, 1981), questions regarding the application of this principle still remain. May a student religious group use a public facility (e.g., a room in the student union or the main thoroughfare of the campus) for devotional activities? May such space be reserved permanently for this purpose?

Admissions
Over the past decade, the number of domestic graduate students has dropped precipitously. Some of the otherwise unfilled places in graduate degree programs have been taken by international students. In fact, without international graduate students, it would be impossible for several universities to justify offering particular courses and conducting certain areas of research. At some institutions, international students predominate particular graduate

programs, although there has been no indication that the overall quality of graduate students has diminished.

As international students dominate the graduate student cohort in some departments, many graduate teaching assistantships are held by nonnative speakers of English. An institution may require that its graduate student instructional staff by proficient in spoken English before being assigned teaching responsibilities (see Chapter 1). Standardized tests of spoken English proficiency have been devised and are in wide usage. Many universities also have instituted training programs for international graduate teaching assistants, involving not only a linguistic component but also a segment on pedagogical skills and a segment on intercultural communication. These are appropriate devices for assuring competent teachers, despite the fact that international students may be singled out.

The setting of admission or enrollment quotas based exclusively on the national origin of students is prohibited by equal opportunity guidelines. While an institution may not deny or limit the admission of students from a specific country, it may establish policies to achieve broad geographical diversification without reference to particular nationalities. For example, it might limit the enrollment of students from one (unspecified) country to no more than 10 percent of the entire student body or to no more than 25 percent of any graduate department.

Asylum
Asylum is an issue that raises the most serious issues for people who are unable to return home because of a "persecution or a well-founded fear of persecution on account of race, religion, nationality, membership in a particular social group, or political opinion" (Refugee Act, 1980). Although it allows serious claimants, pending a decision, to remain in the United States for an extended

period of time, sometimes in excess of a year and permanently if the request is granted, asylum is not a matter to be handled by a counselor or even an experienced international student adviser. Referral to a competent immigration attorney is in order.

Deportation

Deportation is the expulsion of a foreign citizen from the United States after a formal hearing conducted by an immigration judge. A person who is deported may not return to the United States for at least five years and, realistically, may not ever be able to obtain a visa to return. Should international students be issued an Order to Show Cause and Notice of Hearing (the summons to initiate a deportation proceeding), legal help should be sought immediately.

International students who violate the terms of their status may be subject to deportation. The failure to pursue a full course of study or the acceptance of unauthorized employment may cause a student to be deported. Failure to leave the United States after completing the educational program or failure to make timely application for a change of visa classification are also violations of student status and could result in deportation. The willful failure to provide truthful and complete information to the INS is another deportable violation. While these violations could result in deportation, INS officials may choose not to initiate proceedings. Nevertheless, an institution should be aware of the severe legal ramifications that could result from suspending students from classes, hiring students not eligible to be employed, or otherwise placing students in jeopardy of deportation.

Certain criminal activity may subject international students to deportation. Conviction of a violent crime for which a sentence of more than one year may be imposed, whether or not the sentence is actually imposed, and conviction of an offense involving narcotics, including simple possession of a specified quantity of marijuana, also constitute grounds for deportation. The law also looks with displeasure on crimes involving moral turpitude, a legal term without precise definition but which suggests immoral, dishonest, or unscrupulous behavior. Nonimmigrants convicted of two separate crimes involving moral turpitude are deportable; however, conviction of one such crime within five years of entering the United States will result in deportation only if the individuals are actually sentenced to imprisonment for a year or more.

Should a deportation hearing be held and the student found deportable, the immigration judge may grant certain requests for relief from deportation (e.g., permitting the student to leave voluntarily at his/her own expense) rather than order an actual deportation. This relief may enable the student to return to the United States at a later time to continue his/her study.

CONCLUSION

Intricate immigration regulations govern both international students and the institutions enrolling them. They impact virtually every student affairs agency: admissions, counseling, discipline, employment, financial aid, health care, housing, placement, records, recreation, registration, student activities, and the student union. This chapter, while not offering prescriptions for every contingency, outlines those areas in which an institution may have special responsibilities with regard to international students. It also outlines the responsibilities of the students themselves so as to make student affairs professionals aware of the paths students must follow to remain in lawful status and how decisions appropriately taken for domestic students may not always serve the interests of international students. Finally, some examples are offered to provide a living context for immigration and other legal issues for international students and their institutions.

References

Ahmed v. The University of Toledo, 664 F. Supp. 282 (N.D. Ohio 1986), affirmed 822 F.2d 26 (6th Cir. 1987).

Aliens and Nationality, Title 8 Code of Federal Regulations Part 274a (1990).

Bedrosian, A. (Ed.). (1992). *The adviser's manual of federal regulations affecting foreign students and scholars.* Washington, D.C.: National Association for Foreign Student Affairs.

Burak, P.A. (1987). *Crisis management in a cross-cultural setting.* Washington, D.C.: National Association for Foreign Student Affairs.

Civil Rights Act of 1964, 42 USC 2000a (1981 & Supp. 1992).

Employees' Benefits, Title 20 Code of Federal Regulations Part 404.1036 (1991).

Family Educational Rights and Privacy Act of 1974, 20 USC Section 1232g (1990 & Supp. 1992).

Immigration Act of 1990, Pub.L. 101-649.

Immigration and Nationality Act of 1952, 8 USC Section 1101 et seq. (1970 & Supp. 1992).

Immigration and Naturalization Student/Schools Operations Instructions 248.7 (d). (1985).

Immigration Reform and Control Act of 1986, 8 USC Section 1324a, b (Supp. 1992).

National Association for Foreign Student Affairs. (1989). *Code of ethics.* Washington, D.C.: author.

Refugee Act of 1980, Section 208 (a), 8 USC Section 1158 (a), (Supp. 1992) referring to Section 101 (a)(42)(A), 8 USC Section 1101 (a)(42)(A) (1970 & Supp. 1992).

U.S. Department of the Treasury. (1990). *U.S. tax treaties.* Publication 901. Washington, D.C.: Internal Revenue Service.

Widmar v. Vincent, 454 US 263, 278 (1981).

Zikopoulos, M. (Ed.). (1991). *Open doors: 1990/91.* New York: Institute of International Education.

CHAPTER FOUR

Beyond Re-Entry

The Age of the Emerging Global International Student and Scholar

William R. Butler

Over 40 years ago when President Harry S. Truman signed the Fulbright Act into law on August 1, 1946,[1] there was little doubt that international students studying in the United States would return to their home countries after completing their academic studies. Even this author, who began his administrative career at the University of Kansas as a foreign student adviser in 1953, worked with clear-cut understandings and regulations. International students

---

[1] The original act signed in 1946 was Public Law 584 of the 79th Congress, or the Fulbright Act. It was funded from the sale of U.S. war surplus property. Upon depletion of these funds, Senator Fulbright and Representative Wayne Hays sponsored the 1961 Fulbright-Hays Act, officially known as Public Law 256 of the 87th Congress, or the Mutual Educational and Cultural Exchange Act of 1961. It provided for a broader financial base and several other programmatic and technical details. Both acts provided for exchanges of students, faculty, and experts.

returned home. Immigration authorities seldom found it necessary to visit university campuses. Sponsored students, through the Institute of International Education, were enrolled finitely on campuses — usually for one academic year. International students returning to their home countries was not viewed as a major adjustment problem.

Upon completion of a term of study in 1953, placing students in jobs in the United States was rarely considered. Practical training for a short period of time following completion of one's studies was infrequent, and working while enrolled as a student was seldom permitted. International students came from abroad to American universities, completed their academic programs of study, and returned to their home countries. Even the sensitive and complicated cases involving "boy-girl" relationships had little bearing on the defined regulations pertaining to international students returning home. Notably, in 1953 there were fewer than 34,000 students studying in the United States in only 1,600 higher education institutions. International scholars were scarce.

By 1990, events of the world both politically and economically have changed, and the educational philosophy of the United States pertaining to international exchange has expanded. As the nation progresses through the 1990s, it is anticipated that the world's flow of students from other countries will increase above the nearly 400,000 now studying in some 2,900 U.S. institutions. Moreover, the estimated 175,000 faculty and research scholars in the United States will increase as well. International scholar exchange is evolving into an expanded opportunity for technical and scientific collaboration between colleagues and international institutions and is a subject worthy of closer examination for the future.

This chapter examines institutional conditions and opportunities as they exist today in the United States for degree-related employment in the United States prior to international students and scholars returning to their home countries. As the reader will note, the flow of international students and scholars to and from the United States has developed extensively beyond re-entry and immediate return home. We are witnessing the age of the emerging global international student and scholar seeking employment opportunities worldwide.

STUDENT EXCHANGE

In 1967, the Institute of International Education (IIE) conducted a seminar to evaluate the 1946 Fulbright and 1961 Fulbright-Hays Exchange acts and the various campus international programs in effect at that time (Springer, 1967). This seminar followed two decades of experience with student exchange. At the time of the 1967 seminar, slightly over 110,000 international students were then enrolled in some 1,800 U.S. institutions. African representation was 6 percent of those students enrolled; Europe, 14 percent; Latin America, 20 percent; the Middle East, 11 percent; North America, 11 percent; Oceania, 1.5 percent; and Asia, 36.5 percent. There was no mention of international scholars during that seminar (Zikopoulos, 1987, p. 16).

By 1987-88, some two decades later, 356,000 students from abroad studied in over 2,500 U.S. colleges and universities. However, major shifts had occurred by world region of origin in the proportion of international students. The ratio of students from Africa had slightly increased to 8 percent of all international students enrolled; students from Europe had decreased to 11 percent; those from Latin America had dropped to 12.5 percent; and those from the Middle East showed only a moderate increase to 12 percent after a period of substantial growth during the late 1970s and early 1980s. Students from North America had decreased to 4.5 percent; those from Oceania represented only 1 percent; while students from Asia had soared to 51 percent. The flow of students from Asia to the United States had increased substantially and numbers were rising significantly each year (Zikopoulos, 1987).

The 1967 student exchange seminar found the participants both optimistic and pessimistic about the future of student educational exchange. It was feared that greater world isolation might soon occur because of the anticipation that U.S. federal appropriations for the support of international educational exchange would decline. Also, the 1970s might be viewed by Americans as having a sense of "weariness with the idea of rising internationalism, matched by a bitterness toward it, specifically in the developing countries (Springer, 1967, p. 39). Yet, there was also the projection that "knowledge of the world would become more general through large-scale travel and study abroad . . . '' (Springer, 1967, p. 39).

The number of international students studying both in U.S. institutions and, indeed, throughout the world increased continuously in 1968-88. Growth of international students in the United States occurred in all years but one, 1971-72, especially the number of nonsponsored students, i.e., those students who received funding from personal sources rather than government or international organizations (Zikopoulos, 1987, p. 16).

THE INTERNATIONAL SCHOLAR

The line between some advanced international graduate students and some young international researchers is often not sharply defined. International students are generally pursuing a full-time course of study whereas international scholars are engaged primarily in academic research or a well-defined teaching pursuit while possibly enrolling in part-time coursework.

The one area of international exchange which has not been formally quantified since 1974 is the annual census of scholars from abroad. It is estimated there are some 175,000 international scholars with another 50,000 spouses and children on U.S. campuses today and that the growth rate of international scholars has exceeded the rate of international students on many campuses.

Morgan (1989) observes that higher education has been experiencing increases in the number of postdoctoral scholars, especially in the large research institutions, and that their presence appears to be increasing on hundreds of other campuses as well, and should continue through the 1990s. She believes the interests and needs of scholars are different from international students on any campus:

> International scholars come to U.S. institutions to collaborate with a colleague or department in an area of research, to work together and to publish. The specialized research requires access to laboratories, libraries and the opportunity to explore academic research and professional activities (Morgan, 1989, p. 2).

International scholars today may participate in many areas of the entire university, and one can expect that scholars will be even more important to their research universities in the years ahead. In the main, scholars are not enrolled in an academic degree cycle at an institution, and they appear marginal as they are neither students nor faculty. Because greater numbers of scholars are now entering the vast network of international mobility, universities are re-examining their professional services which are available to the scholars and their families. Morgan (1989) observes that in 1985 few universities had specific offices or departments to assist scholars. Efforts to establish these specialized departments increased in the late

1980s, focusing on liaison between the scholars and the universities, the U.S. Immigration and Naturalization Service (INS), the U.S. Information Agency (USIA), and the Department of State (Morgan, 1989).

Moreover, Morgan (1989) asserts that the challenge of the 1990s in international education is to address the unique needs of the visiting exchange visitors, scholars, professors, and researchers through the combined efforts of the individual departments, the institution, and the community.

This new challenge for institutions facing substantial growth in the numbers of international scholars on their campuses requires new thinking by student affairs professionals and other educators about the expanding scholar dimension of international exchange in the 1990s.

Looking beyond the 1990s and preparing for student and scholar exchange in the year 2000, trends indicate that:

° Educational cooperation will continue to increase between both foreign and U.S. universities.
° Decentralization and privatization of the economies throughout the world will continue and will promote further world travel, study, research, and employment opportunities worldwide.
° Increases in the number of international businesses with foreign affiliates will encourage the hiring of international students upon the completion of their academic programs.
° Opportunities for cooperative training and research for international scholars will increase significantly.
° Large-scale research projects have been designed today as bilateral or international joint ventures involving staff members, knowledge, and funding from several countries. Electronic communications will call for new forms of scholarly exchanges, including more very brief visits of members of the international research communities. This trend will grow and, at the same time, offer new challenges and new opportunities for U.S. research universities and their academic and administrative staffs.

CONCERNS ABOUT PLACEMENT
AND RE-ENTRY

If these projections are realized, their impact will significantly affect many institutions. As opportunities increase, there will also be new concerns raised about the adequacy of job placement of international students upon their return home following their study in U.S. colleges and universities. Greater attention will need to be given to the issues relating to international students returning to their home countries after a prolonged period of time, taking into account the changes the international students and the home countries undergo while the students are away.

While re-entry is a clear-cut and well understood objective, it should be examined in light of present world political and economic conditions, trends in U.S. higher education, and political and economic trends in those countries from which the United States draws students and scholars. This author estimates that 65 percent of all nonsponsored international students studying in the United States today will not return immediately to their home countries upon completion of their academic studies. Even in 1967 during the IIE's evaluation seminar, several of the participants estimated that "half of the foreign students don't return home" (Springer, 1967, p. 26). No one really knows the exact number of international students who fail to return home. This statistic was not known in 1967 and it is not known today — not by the IIE, nor the U.S. Department of State, nor the INS.

To clarify the following sections of this chapter, it is essential to pinpoint the main elements which determine the attitudes of international students, the U.S. host institutions, and the U.S. environment at-large. First, we must understand that the enormous increase of the international student population in the United States referred to above, and the large number of nonsponsored students in particular, have changed the rationale for many individuals. Many of them state that they are no longer seeking an education as such. Instead, they state they are seeking training in a special field or skill, and frequently they are willing to invest money and time to acquire such special training.

Also, educators must be acutely aware that international students coming to the United States have either gone through rigorous competition for scholarships or they have taken upon themselves countless efforts to master the paperwork, tests, and other requirements for admission to U.S. institutions. Such efforts are alien to them in terms of their own culture or language or education. It follows then that most international students are highly motivated, are willing to adjust, and they wish to receive maximum benefits from what they consider to be their own investments in professional and personal futures. This explains the increasing demand for practical training as a means of supplementing their educational programs.

If successful, the well-qualified international student is tempted to compete for a position in the United States. It has been the rationale of the United States, however, not to implement programs which will recruit foreign specialists for work in the United States, but rather to assist with development in the students' home countries. Educators on campuses may well face a dilemma: Should they keep the highly gifted student from Somalia from entering their institution's doctoral program because the student cannot possibly continue to work at home? Or, should educators advance the student's training at the risk that the student will elect to remain in the United States? Obviously, educators may be dealing with more questions than they can responsibly answer.

Federal Regulations and Practical Training

The liberalization of federal regulations since May 1987, which permits students the expanded option of seeking practical training not available in their home countries at the end of their academic studies, will likely encourage more students to remain in the United States. Practical training opportunities have permitted students in the F-1 visa classification to engage in part-time and full-time employment for practical training benefits prior to the completion of their studies and up to 12 months full time after degree completion (see Chapter 3).

Great political debate has occurred throughout the past 40 years about the appropriateness of such a federal posture. Indeed, the federal regulations appear to reflect the various changes in the U.S. economy. At the time of this writing, unemployment was 5.5 percent of the nation's working population. Yet, there are people who remain concerned with only "national economic survival," a concept which becomes increasingly obsolete as the world becomes increasingly interdependent. Proponents of job nationalism are concerned that the international student will take a job which should rightfully go to an American and that this is counterproductive to American interests. This xenophobic argument postures the role of international educational exchange as simply that of a monetary exchange for services: tuition money for education.

The Institutional Role Regarding Work and Placement

The liberalization of federal INS regulations in 1987 led to several practical campus problems. International students' employers expressed major concerns about accurately verifying eligibility for work as required by the Immigration Reform and Control Act (IRCA).

Employers remain most unfamiliar with practical training authorization forms. In 1989, the INS began issuing a Standard Work Permit Card in certain states to help employers identify those international students who are eligible to engage in practical training and are, thus, legally able to work. Even with the card and a newly revised *Handbook for Employers*, released in January 1990, there is still confusion in employers' minds as to who may work (Roberts, 1989).

The complexity of interpreting regulations for international students to work is not conducive to American corporations hiring international students for practical training. International student advisers must continue to assist employers regarding practical training regulations and work as well with the departments of career planning and placement.

The international student services office is often the student's only source of information on practical training. Seminars on interpreting employment regulations are currently needed to provide students with accurate information. Written, simplified regulations regarding practical training should be made readily available. School officials need to act on authorization documents quickly to assist the student and the employer. Both the international student services office and the department of career planning and placement should ensure that information about available employment opportunities for international students is available to those students.

The international student services office also needs to provide outreach information to the career planning and placement office to make sure the professional staff targets its efforts toward international students. International students may need special encouragement to use the career office because many international students are not aware that the career office on campus serves students other than U.S. citizens and permanent residents. Resume writing and interviewing technique workshops are of particular importance to international students as they undertake the U.S. job search process (Klein, 1987).

Zsoldos (1989) observes that because the immigration regulations of 1987 permit F-1 students to seek practical training, universities must now expand career counseling services to assist international students in obtaining employment.

Cultural Re-Entry and Adjustment

Much has been written about the need for institutions to assist international students and scholars with cultural re-entry before returning home. For a good many students and scholars, returning home immediately after graduation or completion of research or teaching is a positive experience. For others, however, it can be a cultural shock, requiring several months of personal and professional adjustment.

As Pusch and Loewenthal (1988) observe, "Preparation for going home is as important as preparation for leaving home" (p. iv). These authors recommend that for a successful return, the following should be addressed:

° the recognition of what sojourners are leaving and what has been gained in the new, foreign culture
° the emotional costs of transition
° the value of worrying — anticipating and preparing for difficulties that may occur
° the need for support systems and ways to develop them
° the necessity of developing one's own strategies for going home (p. 3).

Programming, seminars, and advising are among the approaches which should be considered to assist in preparing for the practical aspects of returning home. It is recognized that students who spend prolonged periods of time studying in the United States will begin adjusting to American values and new modes of thinking. As international educators, however, our goal should be that of sharing the American cultural experience and not one of Americanizing international students.

The professional journals detail the various adjustment problems which international students experience as they deal with reverse culture shock — that is, the shock which students and scholars experience upon their return home after being abroad. An issue of the *Advising Quarterly* (Fallgatter, 1987) was devoted to re-entry and provides excellent articles as well as a listing of books and videos available for those interested in addressing these problems.

Prior to returning home, most students will certainly expect substantially more from their existing educational institutions in terms of professional career counseling and job placement services. A trend for the future is best illustrated by the international employment service component of the placement center at Southern Illinois University. This innovative component, opened in 1984, was created to address specifically international students' practical training opportunities and their home country employment and overseas job opportunities. This service publishes a biweekly international jobs bulletin which summarizes vacancies from 175 organizations worldwide and is distributed to students as well as to over 250 universities nationwide (Klein, 1987).

Of the nearly 400,000 international students studying today in the United States, 75 percent of these are estimated to be from developing countries. Most of these students come for study to meet both their own and their country's educational and technical objectives, thereby positioning themselves to meet more effectively their country's staffing needs.

The above statistic raises a particular challenge for American educators who seek to understand and address the special needs of these students. A long-standing problem for students from the developing world who study in the United States has been the transition from academic training in the United States to a professional career in their home countries. Modules and workshops such as those described in *Helping Them Home* (Pusch & Loewenthal, 1988, pp. 9-27) are recommended to assist these students in this process.

The concerns associated with re-entry should not necessarily be solely those of the international student adviser. Other campus student services, in addition to the departments of career planning and placement, may also need to be involved. Professionals from the health service, counseling center, mental health staff, residence halls staff, and campus chaplains may be utilized to assist with the counseling of students who are planning to return to their home countries.

Some educators believe that international students are more likely to experience difficulty returning to their home countries if they have experienced great changes in their values and beliefs while they have been in the United States. Re-entry workshops or exit interviews may be helpful in providing "safe harbors" of support and understanding to the students for their emotional and knowledge-based ideas and values which may have been acquired in the United States.

In a recent seminar, which the author held with several international students who were approaching graduation at the University of Miami, it became apparent that the students, representing 10 different countries, had developed new perspectives on possible lifestyles. They had changed their current lifestyles because of the study abroad experiences in the United States. Most of the students had become more open, and most were more expressive in their manners. Most had been astonished initially by the relaxed manners and approachable ways of their American professors. They had come to the United States to acquire an excellent academic education, but their educational experience was much broader. Most of the students had become more self-reliant as well as independent in their thoughts, values, and behavior.

The students' priorities relative to responsibilities of self versus country were ranked similarly in importance to those of most American students; that is, self-interests and future personal accomplishments were ranked well above the importance of returning home immediately and applying one's newly acquired skills, insights, and talents toward the home country's needs. As one student emphatically stated, "I think about myself first and then my country." The consensus seemed to be that while there were still emotional attachments and loyalty to their home countries, the students seemed to be moving rapidly toward a new status — that of becoming "citizens of the world" — not simply citizens of one's own home country.

Most of the students interviewed intended to use their new educational and leadership skills wherever they could find opportunities for their skills and talents throughout the world. However, they intended to maintain their cultural identities through avenues such as travel and even, perhaps at some future point in time, return to their home countries for employment if such employment opportunities were available to them. Exceptions to not returning home immediately were expressed by those students who were government sponsored and those who felt they had a clear business "contractual" obligation to return home for a specifically defined job. While several students planned to seek employment opportunities at home or in countries outside the United States, many others expressed interest in practical training experiences in the United States for 12-18 months or postgraduate academic opportunities in other U.S. universities. These students' "best guess" was that the United States would offer them far greater professional and graduate opportunities than would be true in their own countries.

All the students thought the University of Miami should be doing far more for them in "opening employment doors," both from a practical training perspective as well as a long-time professional employment perspective. Students feared that employers would not hire an international student if they felt the student would be required to return home in one year. The suggestion was made that the term practical training be changed in the federal law to work authorization, the feeling being that somehow employers would then be more willing to hire international students.

Ultimately, international students and international scholars must accept responsibility for the successes or failures of their educational experiences, and return home or enter into a new professional life in the United States or some other place in the world. (Two publications listed in the references, *The Advising Quarterly*, Fallgatter, 1987, and *Going Home,* Denny, 1986, are excellent resources for addressing these subjects.)

The following resources are also suggested for the reader's consideration:

- ° associating with institutional alumni through American university clubs or American university associations worldwide
- ° affiliating with institutional alumni groups since universities, themselves, are good sources for alumni contacts
- ° visiting U.S. Embassies Information Service, which has offices worldwide
- ° subscribing to job listing newsletters such as those for African and Latin American countries which are published by the Intergovernmental Committee for Migration in Washington, D.C.
- ° building personal networks with former professors

° building personal networks with professional associations
° visiting home country embassies
° visiting binational Fulbright commissions worldwide.

All are excellent resources which can be of personal and professional service to both students and scholars.

THE UNITED STATES AND RUSSIA: AGENTS OF SOCIALIZATION

In an indepth interview with a Jamaican student who had recently completed the Master of Arts degree in the University of Miami's Graduate School of International Studies, the contrast between the educational systems in the United States and Russia was striking. Prior to her studies in the United States, this student had received a scholarship to study as a Third World student at the Patrice Lumumba University in Moscow. Since 1960, this Russian institution has offered educational training to thousands of students from the developing world. The graduate student's thesis was a follow-up study of several Jamaican students' re-entry to their home country after completing their academic studies in Russia. This fascinating study not only highlights the cultural difficulties which the students faced upon their return home, but also touches on the world's political struggles which concern individuals from Third World countries (Ewart-Simon, 1989).

In another recent interview with an educational official from Syria who was visiting the University of Miami campus, this author asked, "How many students from Syria study in the United States and in Russia?" The reply was that there were approximately 5,000 Syrian students studying medicine and engineering in Russia whereas only 2,000 were studying in the United States, those being in computer sciences engineering and other high technology areas. When asked why there was such a difference, the Syrian educator replied, "Students studying in the United States often have great difficulty — when they experience the 'good life' in the United States, it is very difficult for them to return home. Students often leave Syria and do not return.'' When further queried as to why students studying in Russia have fewer difficulties returning home, he replied, "There is less personal freedom in Russia, so there are fewer adjustment problems.''

A final question was asked of the Syrian educator, "How do people feel when a student from Syria is permitted to study in the United States?" His reply was, "There are feelings of joy and feelings of sadness because we know the student will receive a very good education. But he will probably not return home."

The conditions facing Syrian students are, indeed, similar to those faced by many other students from Third World and developing countries. In their home countries, the "creature comforts" found in the United States are often unavailable. For example, the 30,000 students studying in the United States from the People's Republic of China have no automobiles in China nor do they have driving opportunities at home. In the United States, however, many relinquish their bicycles in favor of old, inexpensive cars.

THE BRAIN DRAIN

Countries such as Syria, Malaysia, China, and other countries throughout Africa and Asia will likely become more restrictive in the future in granting their undergraduates permission to study in the United States. The opportunities, however, for international scholars should increase since this area of exchange is receiving greater attention today. Several developing countries are now adopting the philosophy that study abroad should be restricted to graduate study only and that these study opportunities should be reserved for the highly technical areas. Usually the undergraduate education in one's home country lessens the risk of dramatic value shifts while studying in the United States at a younger and more impressionable age. Undergraduates who continue for several degrees are less likely to return home after spending many years in the United States.

Germany has attempted to address the issue of brain drain by placing fairly strict regulations on those foreign students who elect to study in Germany with German funding. If they decide to remain in Germany, they must, as a rule, pay back what they receive. One particular German scholarship program was introduced primarily for students from developing countries, especially in Africa, where Germany has been paying for most of the students who study abroad. Today, there are German grants for Africans who elect not to come to Germany for study but, instead, elect to study in another African country. This program, entitled Sur Place Scholarship Program, allows, for example, a student from Kenya to study at a university in Nigeria on a German government grant (Bode, 1990).

Another German project, called the Sandwich Study, provides, for example, German scholarship funding for doctoral students in North Africa or in Latin America. Thus, a student in North Africa might elect to study in an Egyptian university under a doctoral committee in Cairo which would include a German professor from Bonn or Hamburg. The best students might spend six months in Cairo and then do part of their dissertation research in Bonn or Hamburg for one year. The student would then return to Cairo to write the dissertation and return to Germany to do the final "finetuning" under the German professor. The student would eventually receive the doctorate at the University of Cairo. These students essentially remain in their home educational systems while being influenced greatly by German higher education (Bode, 1990).

The prospect that the brain drain will likely increase throughout the 1990s is real. Moreover, students from developing countries with inadequate economic and technical opportunities at home will likely seek those opportunities wherever they exist worldwide. As was observed in the IIE evaluation seminar in 1967, "The brain drain flow is in the direction of the resources, the intellectual excitement" (Springer, 1967, p. 26).

Frankel's 1967 solution (cited in Springer, 1967) to the brain drain problem is just as relevant today. He advocates the spreading of the intellectual and economic stimuli beyond national borders to create multinational enterprises in many places. Frankel observes,

> That the cure for the brain drain is to circulate brains, and to make some international arrangements that allow for this. International exchanges must be viewed as major instruments for dealing with what (he) regarded as the central problem in development — the equitable distribution of human resources and talent, particularly those special talents we know as leadership. This is a central problem in getting the world a little bit more equitably balanced than it is now. Intellectual exchange and international education is a major instrument for dealing with this problem (Springer, 1967, p. 30).

Yet there are serious worldwide political and economic issues and concerns which should give us pause today about encouraging international students and scholars not to return to their home countries. Schieffer (1989) claims attention is given to the current terminology which illuminates the complexities of nonreturning individuals. Such terms as nonreturn do not do justice to the brain drain phenomenon which he defines as the "migration of talent" and describes the movement of people, skilled and unskilled, from their countries of origin to new countries either temporarily or permanently.

The migration of talent from one's home country to countries which hold brighter political and economic opportunities is not new. A 1966 study of Chilean professionals identified four factors which motivated them to migrate to the United States:

° professional advancement
° better remuneration
° greater recognition of technical or scientific work
° wider opportunities for research (Olivas & Perez, 1966).

Berger (1988) observes that the recent movement of British faculty to American higher education institutions is "... part of a migration that may be [the largest single influx into this country from a single source] since Jewish professors were forced to leave Germany and Austria in the 1930s "(p. A1).

Moreover, as the education of students and scholars in the United States has increased so dramatically during the past 40 years, so too has the migration of talent worldwide. It is estimated that over one million students are studying in countries other than their own today, but so too has the number of countries substantially increased to which students go (Selvaratnam, 1985, p. 310).

Schieffer (1989) states that colleges and universities cannot "distance themselves from the implications of the migration of talent." He believes the future of educational exchange may well rest with the respect and sensitivity the U.S. colleges and universities hold for the needs and desires of nations, as well as the needs and desires of individual students and scholars. He concludes:

> In the past, the postsecondary community viewed migration of talent issues as largely political and therefore the concern of the

government. However, some members of the postsecondary community now suggest that certain obligations are implicit when postsecondary institutions espouse the principles of educational exchange. Foremost among these, perhaps, is the return of the sojourner to the home country, thus completing the exchange cycle and securing for future students and scholars the opportunity to participate in international educational exchanges (Schieffer, 1989, p. 15).

It should be kept in mind as well that the migration of talent has indeed become a two-way movement. American scholars have become professors on many distinguished faculties around the world, and artists of all kinds are found in operas, orchestras, and art galleries from Copenhagen to Milano to Tokyo. Many of these Americans made contact first as grantees under an exchange program, just like many international scholars on our campuses who do not return to their native countries. The academic community and the business world usually regard such migrants of advanced standing rather as "bridge builders" to promote relations with their home countries. Governments abroad, and those of less developed countries in particular, as well as the U.S. administration, however, assess the loss to the home country.

MUTUAL UNDERSTANDING AND GLOBAL EDUCATION

When the Fulbright Act was passed in 1946, Senator J. William Fulbright was concerned about the advice scientist Albert Einstein gave at the time of the invention of the atomic bomb. Fulbright (1989) recalls in his book, *The Price of Empire,* "Einstein made his famous and perceptive statement about the essentiality for man to develop a new way of thinking about international relations, failing which, we would be faced with incalculable catastrophe" (p. 193). Fulbright (1989) continues on to say that everyone wants peace and that

> One thing that gives me some hope is the ethos that underlies the educational exchange program. That ethos, in sum, is the belief that international relations can be improved, and the danger of war significantly reduced, by producing generations of leaders, who through the experience of educational understanding of other peoples' cultures — why they operate as they do, why they think as they do, why they react as they do — and of the differences among these cultures. It is possible — not very probable, but possible — that people can find in themselves, through intercultural education, the ways and means of living together in peace (p. 194).

Fulbright's belief in the educational experience which provides the often forgotten side benefit of "mutual understanding" should not be considered lightly when one ponders as does Lau (1984), author of *The World at Your Doorstep,* that one-third to one-half of the world's top positions in politics, business, education, and the military will be filled in the next 25 years by foreign students attending colleges and universities in the United States. In short, among the nearly 400,000 international students studying in U.S. institutions today, the nation can expect to educate between 33 percent to 50 percent of tomorrow's global leaders (Rentz, 1987, p. 10).

Even though a widely held view is that undergraduates should remain in their home countries, it is clear that American undergraduate education is not and will not be static. It, too, is changing. As Boyer (1987) emphasizes,

> For 350 years, it [American education] has shaped its program in response to the changing social and economic context. As we

look to a world whose contours remain obscure, we conclude the time has come to reaffirm the undergraduate experience and, in so doing, help students move from competence to commitment and be of service to the neighborhoods, the nation, and the world (p. 297).

For the most part, the American higher education experience does just that — it provides both a superior academic learning experience within the classroom and it provides superior opportunities for the development of leadership experiences and skills outside the classroom. These extra class opportunities are some of the most unique and positive aspects about American higher education. These opportunities and the commitments to service and leadership which students develop are seldom found in other countries of the world, especially in Third World, developing countries.

CLOSING THOUGHTS

It is fitting that the author end this chapter by citing the personal experiences of his son. Following Michael Butler's undergraduate career at Eckerd College in 1979, he elected to teach English in a Japanese public high school in Takamatsu, Japan. In 1980, he enrolled in Sophia University in Tokyo and studied the Japanese language while teaching English in his off hours to Japanese children and businessmen. After three years in Japan, he then ventured to Taipei, Taiwan, in 1982 where he continued with language studies, this time undertaking Mandarin Chinese and Taiwanese. He has been in Taiwan eight years now and has advanced to the level of teaching Taiwanese teachers how to teach English in a private language school in Taipei. He also is pursuing his business interests following his participation for several years in a Chinese import-export business in Taipei.

Butler has a deep commitment to the Pacific rim countries. His interests have pulled him culturally and economically to Asia. Yet he makes short trips annually to the United States to keep alive his family and American roots. While he remains a U.S. citizen, he has become more a "citizen of the world." This is not unlike so many other young internationals who, as Frankel (cited in Springer, 1967) suggests, elect to "circulate brains" through the pursuit of professional, cultural, and economic opportunities outside their home countries without giving up their home country citizenship.

Will the 1990s motivate even more internationally minded students and scholars to acquire essential language skills and other technical talents to pursue professional careers in countries other than their own? This author believes so. Although only time will tell, this author believes that such experiences will be more commonplace for both U.S. students and scholars as well as international students and scholars in the years ahead.

A new generation of political, economic, and educational leadership is being experienced worldwide. Countries which have been closed are now open. Countries which were once divided are now being unified. World travel restrictions are being relaxed. There is a mass movement of people occurring throughout the world which fosters openness and the further enhancement of political and economic freedoms. Such changes will encourage the educational and economic transfer of scientific and high-technology knowledge and skills in the future in ways undreamed of in the years immediately behind us.

The unique opportunities for a global education and the global flow of talent in the 1990s are upon us. We have entered an age "beyond re-entry" in this period of the global job seeking international student and scholar. Seizing these opportunities will enable us to fulfill more fully Senator Fulbright's educational exchange vision of "mutual understanding."

As our nation approaches the 21st century and speculates about each of our institutional concerns for the job placement and re-entry of international students and scholars, the following should be considered:

■ The number of international students and scholars who will seek American higher educational opportunities will continue to increase throughout the 1990s.

■ Many more international students and scholars are expected to travel abroad and study, teach, and perform research abroad.

■ The number of international students who will seek practical training opportunities upon completion of their studies and then seek long-term professional job opportunities will increase throughout the 1990s.

■ Greater emphasis and importance will be placed on campus student services for greater sensitivity and international scholars, e.g., part-time employment, career planning, job placement, advising, counseling and campus-wide extra class programming geared to the international student and scholar.

■ Employers in the United States will offer additional job opportunities to international students and scholars throughout the 1990s because of the shortage of individuals with both technological skills and foreign language skills.

■ INS regulations will continue to permit international students to work in American companies.

■ The number of students and scholars who elect to work in countries other than their own will increase. This flow of talent will likely follow the rise and fall of political, economic, and technological events worldwide.

■ The concept of brain drain will continue to be a concern in terms of both the nonreturn of individuals to their home countries as well as the temporary migration of talent throughout the world.

■ There will be new economic and political opportunities and innovative approaches for the recruitment of students and scholars to the United States from Third World countries.

■ Because of the interdependence of countries worldwide, employment barriers for skilled and professional talent will likely be relaxed.

■ There may be a modest reversal in the 1990s in the outflow of skilled professionals from certain countries because of the creative recruitment strategies being put into place to bring back home students and scholars (e.g., South Korea, Taiwan, and the Peoples Republic of China).

References

Berger, J. (1988, November 22). British brain drain enriches U.S. colleges. *New York Times*, p. A-1.
Boyer, E.L. (1987). *College: The undergraduate experience in America*. New York: Harper and Row.

Bode, C. (1990). DADD Annual Report. Bonn, Germany: German Academic Exchange Service.

Denny, M. (1986). *Going home: A workbook for reentry and professional integration.* Washington, D.C.: National Association for Foreign Student Affairs.

Ewart-Simon, A.M.R. (1989). Educating for the future: Third-world scholars in the Soviet Union. Unpublished master's thesis, University of Miami.

Fallgatter, J. (Ed.).(1987). Reentry. *The Advising Quarterly.*

Fulbright, J.W. (1989). The price of empire. New York: Pantheon Books.

Klein, F.O. (1987). Job hunting from the U.S. *The Advising Quarterly, 2.*

Lau, L. (1984). *The world at your doorstep.* Downers Grove, Ill.: Intervarsity Press.

Morgan, L. (1989). International exchange scholars: Today and in the 1990s. Unpublished report. University of Miami.

Olivas, S.G., and Perez, J.R. (1966). *The emigration of high level manpower: The case of Chile.* Washington, D.C.: Organization of American States.

Pusch, M.D., and Loewenthal, N. (1988). *Helping them home: A guide for leaders of professional integration and reentry workshops.* Washington, D.C.: National Association for Foreign Student Affairs.

Rentz, M.D. (1987, February 16). Diplomats in our backyard. *Newsweek*, p. 10.

Roberts, M.A. (1989, October 2). *Interpreter releases: Report and analysis of immigration and nationality law.* Washington, D.C.: Federal Publications, Inc.

Schieffer, K. (1989, December). Migration of talent. Unpublished paper. Washington, D.C.: National Association for Foreign Student Affairs.

Selvaratnam, V. (1985). The international flow of scholars and students: A vehicle for cross-cultural understanding, international, and global development? *International Journal of Educational Development,* 5(4), 307-23.

Springer, G.P. (1967). *A report on the Fulbright-Hays student exchange program seminar.* New York: Institute of International Education.

Zikopoulos, M. (Ed.).(1987). *Open doors: 1987-88.* New York: Institute of International Education.

Zsoldos, I. (1989). Project assists career planning for international students. *NAFSA Newsletter,* 4(1), 18.

CHAPTER FIVE

Working with International Students On Our Campuses

Carmen G. Neuberger

In order to realize the potential enrichment that international students bring to U.S. colleges and universities, it is important to understand this unique clientele and make provisions for meeting its needs within each institution's context. To accomplish this, carefully drafted campus-wide policies reflecting institutional mission are critical. These policies are as important in student affairs as they are in the academic area. The catalog and faculty handbook are usually well-accepted resources. On the nonacademic side, administrator and student handbooks do not always exist and when they do, they may fail to address important policies. Problems encountered by international students can often be prevented through publication of a handbook addressing their concerns and referring them to resources which explain rules and the rationale for them.

Quann and Associates (1979) edited a handbook on policies and procedures for admissions officers and registrars which lists possible effects of not having a policy on international educational exchange. These include

° Well-meaning attempts of individual faculty with enthusiastic international interests but no knowledge of how to develop them result in invitations to campus of international scholars or students which could be costly for both participants and institution.
° Students and staff members may leave the institution to seek other outlets for their international interests.
° Unqualified and poorly financed international students may be admitted and enrolled in possible violation of federal law and institutional requirements
° Students and faculty may have unrealistic expectations and may become involved in serious academic, financial, or legal difficulties.

This chapter addresses international student admissions, housing, and financial matters — areas which frequently fall within the purview of student affairs. Policies in these areas are not easily defined and disseminated. First, admissions standards and recruitment strategies are necessarily subjective and seldom shared with candidates for admission. Second, except for institutions where on-campus housing is mandatory or there is a housing lottery (which is the most common tool for assigning housing), procedures for choosing various housing options on and off campus are rarely published in detail. Third, the true cost of an education in the United States is difficult to assess because students' lifestyles are different. Many schools fail to provide accurate and reasonable estimates of educational and living expenses in the region of the chosen campus and the extent to which any financial aid is available to international students prior to enrollment.

INTERNATIONAL STUDENT ADMISSIONS

The task of solving the serious adjustment and economic problems of international students who need extensive advising and devising remedies for difficult situations when institutional policy is not clearly spelled out often falls upon the shoulders of the international student adviser and other student affairs administrators. Beginning with admission, continuing through arrival and orientation, and peaking with housing and developmental activities, meeting the unique financial and social needs of international students poses a special challenge to student service providers. As the primary representatives and interpreters of institutional policy and as professionals who take seriously the mandate to help promote multiculturalism, student affairs professionals truly believe that successful international exchange education adds a unique dimension to campus life. From a wider perspective, we are convinced that it contributes to peace and understanding in the world.

In *The Admissions Strategist*, a special issue on recruiting international students published by the College Board, Peterson (1987) gives six commandments for a well-conceived institutional policy on international student admissions. Such a policy should

° Ensure that the institution's international educational exchange activities are consistent with its mission and priorities.
° Enable the institution to be effective and consistent in targeting, admitting, retaining, educating, and serving international students.
° State explicitly international student admissions goals and priorities; academic and personal characteristics of students to be sought; geographic areas to be emphasized, or balance sought; target population levels as a proportion of the student body in the institution or in particular programs.

° Once in place, dictate operational choices to be made: allocation of resources for recruitment, support services, faculty and staff development; coordination of existing services.
° Enable the institution to meet established standards of good practice.
° Provide the basis for ongoing assessment of the international student program

The Field Service Program of the National Association for Foreign Student Affairs (1978) lists seven questions institutions should ask when reviewing its international student admissions program:

■ What academic objectives of individual international students can the institution satisfy?

■ At what levels of admission and for what periods of time is the institution prepared to educate international students (undergraduate versus graduate students; special student status)?

■ What optimum number of international students can reasonably be served?

■ What specific services to international students is the institution prepared to offer or develop (such as housing assistance, English language instruction, or orientation)? Is there an adequately staffed international student adviser's office to coordinate these services?

■ What resources are available for financial assistance?

■ What contribution does the institution expect international students to make to the campus and the community?

■ Can an effective international student program be developed without compromising present or future educational goals and standards of the institution? (p. 17)

In addition, the National Association for Foreign Student Affairs (NAFSA) urges policy makers to consider what cultural mix (i.e., ratio) of U.S. and international students is appropriate and feasible for the institution as a whole, for the various departments, and for the different academic levels. A decision to concentrate on one or more countries or continental areas or to seek broad geographical representation must also be made. Students' academic and socioeconomic backgrounds are also important considerations. Once again, these decisions must be made on the basis of objectives for the program and financial support available.

Once a sound admissions policy is in place, recruitment strategies should be developed. In addition to guidelines already mentioned, other strategies include:

° Admissions materials should be thorough, complete, and clearly written; they should be sensitive to candidates' unfamiliarity with U.S. education and lack of proficiency in English
° The international admissions process should be conducted by personnel who are trained and competent in interpreting international education records
° The admissions program should be coordinated with academic and student affairs, providing for regular contact and sharing of information.

Once policy has been formulated, the next item of importance is planning. The presence of over 370,000 international students on our campuses, although only 2.5 percent of the total student population in the United States, can be one of our richest resources. Elkins (1989) states that international students spent an estimated $2.25 billion in one year on living expenses. This figure does not include tuition, fees, books, travel, or dependents' expenses. A long-range strategic plan for international educational exchange is critical in order to reduce the risk of failure for both institution and student and to realize benefits. These benefits range from enhanced diversity and an enriched cultural climate on campus and in the community to improved fund raising based on the international dimension in campus programs, and strengthened campus-community relations through existing international interests of the local population. Limbird and Owen (1987), in the College Board's *Admissions Strategist*, state that a positive climate cultivated through identification and nurturance of a network of personnel, services, and programs can be created through careful planning.

ENGLISH LANGUAGE AND FINANCIAL REQUIREMENTS OF INSTITUTIONS

English language proficiency is a sensitive area for international student admissions officers to assess once the process for evaluating credentials earned at secondary and postsecondary institutions abroad has been established. Determining academic eligibility must be reviewed in conjunction with the English language ability of candidates for admission. Unlike the SAT and ACT tests, the TOEFL (Test of English as a Foreign Language) is not as widely accepted a predictor for success in a given academic program. A more personalized evaluation of requirements specific to an institution should be compared with the international student's overall record. TOEFL scores must be supplemented by other information such as careful credential evaluation and the international student's field of proposed study. Areas of weakness such as English writing skills or listening comprehension should be noted, and any requirement for additional study and proficiency testing in the English language must be carefully spelled out in admissions communication with each student prior to and subsequent to the decision to apply and enroll.

Last but not least in the area of admissions and recruitment is the important matter of detailing financial requirements and determining the adequacy of resources presented by an international student at time of application. The primary institutional responsibility in this area is the provision of accurate, current, and realistic information on costs of attendance at that institution and sources for any financial aid available to international students. The international student adviser is the traditional liaison with sponsoring governmental and private agencies and is relied upon to keep abreast of world events which might have an impact on students from other countries. As the person most knowledgeable about a student's financial status, the international student adviser interprets sponsors' funding requirements and restrictions to the home institution and advises students on permission to work and the ability to incur debt or receive aid from other sources. Foreign exchange transfer rules and regulations must be met by citizens of those countries, and institutional reminders for application are often necessary on an annual basis. Currency restrictions and current exchange rates for U.S. dollars are other factors to be considered. Communication among admissions, financial aid, bursar, and the international student services office is crucial in assuring the legality and propriety of various financial sources for international students. When these students are accompanied by dependents, the funding questions become much more complex.

While making plans to meet their financial obligations prior to departure for a U.S. college or university, international students need as much information as possible

from the host school to meet the documentation
requirements for immigration entry papers. Official,
written statements of awards detailing support and
accompanying responsibilities such as taxes owed,
pay-back or work expected should always be provided.
Sponsors are sometimes willing to deposit a bond with the
school to guarantee that students will not become a burden
financially during their period of study in the United States.
Some colleges and universities expect international
students to provide affidavits or certificates of support when
using their own financial resources. In recent years, a
dwindling pool of funds from outside sources has made it
necessary for these institutions to reserve the bulk of their
funds for U.S.-born students. To assist international
students, financial planning assistance is also available
through the Overseas Educational Advising Centers
operated in close cooperation with the U.S. Information
Services in most capital cities throughout the world. A
directory of these advising centers is available through the
College Entrance Examination Board in New York City and
through U.S. embassies and consulates.

In its publication, *Entering Higher Education in the
United States: A Guide to Admissions and Financial
Planning for Students from Other Countries,* the College
Board (1989) offers financial advice for international
students:

° Students should obtain accurate estimates of expenses from
the institutions they wish to enter. If ranges of costs are
given, use the high figure for planning purposes.
° Add 10 percent to the estimated amount for unexpected
expenses.
° If students are receiving fellowships or assistantships, they
should not convert the U.S. dollar amount into their own
currency and imagine they will be comfortable. The cost of
living in the United States is high.

° It is essential to have health insurance and a source of
  emergency funds either in the United States or another
  country.
° Students should have medical, dental, and optical
  check-ups at home and should correct any problems before
  leaving.
° Students should not come to the United States until they are
  certain their first year's expenses are fully covered, and that
  there is at least a reasonable prospect of meeting their
  expenses for the entire period of study without depending
  on employment.
° Students should have money transferred from home at
  regular intervals.
° When they arrive, students should have on hand enough
  money to cover the first few months. They should
  remember they will probably spend more during this period
  than later.
° It is important to keep to a budget.
° Students should think twice before buying unnecessary
  merchandise.
° It is important that students seek help from the international
  student adviser of their college or university as soon as they
  begin to have financial difficulties or any other adjustment
  concerns.

When bringing spouses and children, it is even more
critical that the student prove sufficiency of funds. There
is a greater likelihood for financial problems to develop
when a student is accompanied by family members.

HOUSING NEEDS

While research and resource books on admitting
international students are readily available through the
American Association of Collegiate Registrars and
Admissions Officers (AACRAO), the College Board's

Office of International Education, the Institute of International Education (IIE), and the National Association for Foreign Student Affairs (NAFSA), information on international students' housing needs, apart from international living centers, is minimal. Goodwin and Nacht (1983) conclude that the increased presence of international students has caught U.S. college and university officials unprepared for the "economic, educational, political and organizational issues of large numbers of foreign students on their campuses" (p. 40).

To promote the interaction and cultural exchange a residential campus offers, the efforts of an integrated residence hall staff and program are necessary. NAFSA has published a sourcebook (Reiff, 1986) in which housing personnel are encouraged to cooperate and collaborate with international student advisers to enhance international interchange. Stating that "substantive, consistent, and meaningful international interchange does not automatically happen," Reiff (1986) calls for "a concerted effort; a commitment to attain specific objectives; most of all, it requires knowledgeable trained professionals" (p. 2). Training in intercultural communication, American cultural patterns, and culture shock are areas which must be treated in depth for residence hall staff to understand and encourage the sharing of "ideas and feelings, clarifying values, and enhancing human relations through contact with people of varying backgrounds" (Reiff, 1986, p. 2).

Because international students' cultural beliefs and behaviors vary considerably, it is impossible to give professionals detailed training on the many nationalities present on their campuses, apart from such general notions as the formality and rituals in the daily life of foreign cultures. Training sessions usually focus on understanding how Americans are oriented and the lifestyles and things which are valued in the United States. Not only is it appropriate for staff members born here to study their upbringing and culture, but these sessions also assist them to develop tolerance and appreciation of international students who act and react in different ways. Examples of common daily "problems" with international students in residence halls reflect differences in their dominant cultures compared with U.S. behavior patterns. According to Artman (1986), these are

° The student who stays in the room and will not mix
° The student who wants to live off campus with others from his/her country
° The student whose cooking odors sicken other residents
° The male student who will not confide in a female staff member
° The student whose roommate resents "borrowing" of personal items
° The student who refuses to keep appointments
° The student who does not participate in competitive activities
° The student whose religious worship or ritual offends roommates
° The student who spends his/her housing allowance on a new car.

Residence hall staff can help roommates and residents be more accepting and patient while working with international students to help educate them on American cultural patterns since neither culture is primarily right nor necessarily wrong. Providing a living environment that is comfortable and companionable takes much energy, constant attention, and a commitment to expanding the world of students.

Responsibilities that international students can be expected to meet are listed in NAFSA's (1979) standards statement. These include:

° To strive to understand and tolerate host country's
  educational and cultural setting, including standards of
  conduct, law, respect for others, honesty, and integrity
° To respect others' rights of self-determination
° To participate as fully as possible in the life of the host
  university or country, in joint and cooperative ventures of
  an educational, social, or cultural nature with other
  international students as well as U.S. students
° To accept responsibility for making the most of the
  international educational exchange program to gain widest
  possible support and involvement.

Solmon and Young (1987) examine the general goals, characteristics, and attitudes of international students in relation to their U.S. peers through data collected during the Cooperative Institutional Research Program (CIRP) surveys of first-time freshmen in American colleges and universities conducted in 1972 and 1982. These surveys are administered annually by the University of California at Los Angeles under continuing sponsorship of the American Council on Education. Enrollment by regions and rationale for these choices provided by Higher Education General Information Survey (HEGIS) data collected by the Center for Statistics are also included.

According to their findings, the age for entering nonresident foreign freshmen has increased by 25 percent in the age 16 or less category; 25 percent in the 17-19 year old category; and decreased close to 50 percent in the 20 year or older category, reflecting similar but smaller changes in national norms. Female nonresident international freshmen have increased from 25 to 40 percent of the total. Marital status has changed in a corresponding fashion with 99.5 percent of the nonresident international freshmen not currently married in 1982 compared with 96.4 percent in 1972, the equivalent national norms being 99.1 percent in 1982 and 97.7 percent in 1972.

Graduate student data is not as readily available. These students increased by 6 percent over the previous year while undergraduate international students decreased by 4 percent according to the 1988-89 edition of *Open Doors* (Institute of International Education, 1989). It can be assumed that more of these students are apt to be married and, if married, accompanied by dependents. Their needs are quite different from the traditional-aged undergraduate student.

In addition, Friedman (1987) states that students often extend their stay beyond the regular time period of U.S.-born full-time graduate students to complete their course of study so as to include teaching and practical training. Practical training consists of temporary off-campus employment in the student's field of study. This training is approved either as follow-up to a brief practicum requirement or as a separate, usually not more than 12-month work experience which is not available in the student's home country. Most of the residence halls for graduate or older students are supported by minimal staff, offering basic room and optional board programs similar to 1960-70 laissez-faire and European models.

For those students who are married and bring their dependents, orientation to the United States is important for the entire family to ensure academic success for the student and cultural adjustment for the family. Transportation, convenience to stores, safety and security, schools for the children, and recreational facilities are concerns. Beyond these basic needs is the necessary ability to communicate and function in a culture alien to their own, which is most likely far more conservative, sheltered, and less developed than the United States. Staff members trained to work with families, knowledgeable about child care and changing roles of women and men are required.

Many institutions with international students establish an international living center or international house on or near campus. While sometimes criticized as international student ghettos, these centers can provide valuable developmental opportunities for academic, social, and cross-cultural programs as well as valuable orientation for these students to their new environment. "Ghettoizing" is minimized when the population is controlled so that U.S.-born residents outnumber foreign-born and the living arrangement is optional rather than assigned. College or university staff overseeing this facility must be attuned to isolation issues and the comfort of the familiar when international students socialize only with residents of the international house.

On the positive side, personal ties for international students which often last for their entire stay in the United States often begin in this more accepting, informal living facility. As a focus for multicultural activities for the entire campus, according to Stern, Tower, and Doney (1986), the international living center can serve "as a catalyst for integrating academic interest in international affairs with the social and personal interest of the students" (p. 12). U.S.-born students who are enrolled in international affairs academic programs or who have lived and traveled abroad, are often attracted to these centers to further their own development. A well-planned and implemented program and staff can achieve a good balance and bring to the campus many of the benefits of a unified and goal-oriented international exchange program.

STUDENT SERVICES RELATED TO INTERNATIONAL STUDENTS

Just as higher education institutions are reluctant to enroll only U.S. students who have the individual or familial financial assets to afford the entire cost, so, too, do they seek international students from the spectrum of classes, from privileged to self-made. As a result, some of these international students have financial needs comparable to those of their U.S. counterparts. In addition, because of strict U.S. financial aid policies, legal restrictions on the ability of international students to hold certain paid positions and the instability of world economics and politics, the financial problems of these students are often quite complex. In *Policy and Practice in the Administration of Foreign Student Finances,* NAFSA (1983) suggests that the most effective cure for this ailment is prevention. Comprehensive procedures are outlined as follows:

■ Admissions
   ° Accurate, up-to-date information on costs
   ° Any financial aid available
   ° Careful screening of financial documentation

■ International Student Services Office
   ° Orientation on U.S. banking, personal budgeting skills, and other financial matters
   ° Invitation to discuss potential financial problems before they materialize
   ° Communication with each sponsoring agency
   ° Liaison with student accounts and other campus offices regarding international student finances

■ Financial Aid Office
   ° Identification of financial aid resources available to international students
   ° Verification procedures for international student eligibility

It is the external factors in various countries of origin which are much more difficult to control and deal with. When economic crises occur, private institutions and, in rare cases, state legislatures have provided tuition and fee waivers and increased on-campus employment opportunities until these economic difficulties can be resolved. Fund-raising drives by alumni and community, contributions by U.S. corporations in return for consultation services of students regarding their home countries, short- and long-term loans are also employed, with verification of students' ability to repay.

In *Entering Higher Education in the United States: A Guide to Admissions and Financial Planning for Students from Other Countries,* the College Board (1989) emphasizes the importance of careful and realistic financial planning for prospective international students. Outlining expenses such as travel, English language courses, orientation programs, tuition and fees, room and board, books and supplies, health insurance, incidental expenses and summer costs, and married student dependent support, it covers comprehensively all the areas for which students will need money. Sample budget forms, obligations of private sponsors, transfer of funds, currency restrictions, banking services, and even money needed upon arrival are addressed. A description of the types of financial aid available for study in the United States, application procedures and sources of such aid both within and without the United States are noted. Also included in this publication is a summary of advice experienced international students give to those just beginning to plan for study in the United States. It is practical and peer oriented.

English language instruction is usually the first classroom experience for an international student. Its importance to the success of the institution's exchange program should not be underestimated. NAFSA's *Standards and Principles for Professional Staff and Volunteers* (1979) includes specific responsibilities for teachers of English as a second language. These are:

° Acquire adequate training and proficiency in this special academic
° Offer patience and understanding necessary to student success but not undue sympathy which may jeopardize academic standards
° Instruct in all aspects of the English language, including acculturation and other knowledge beyond vocabulary and grammar
° Interpret to faculty and administrators the realities of language acquisition, including linguistic areas which reasonably can be mastered and those which are highly unlikely
° Communicate professionally and confidentially to international student adviser any knowledge received of a significant student problem when it is in the student's best interest to do so
° Encourage and refer international students to appropriate agencies for assistance
° Provide training and liaison to campus agencies in assisting students to overcome language handicaps
° Maintain professional development in language acquisition and linguistics as well as other aspects of international educational exchange.

Personal and cross-cultural counseling are services often relegated to the international student adviser. With the heavy administrative workload imposed by INS requirements, these advisers do not have the time nor the credentials to handle deep-seated psychological and physical problems. The institution's counselors and student health care providers should be prepared to handle the unique as well as more commonplace counseling and health services for international students (see Chapter 3).

CONCLUSION

International educational exchange is growing in importance in higher education and as enrollments of international students in U.S. institutions increase, so must our abilities to meet their unique needs. Once a college or university makes a commitment to international education and allocates resources for this purpose, institution-wide principles applying to admissions, English programs, international student services, U.S. study abroad programs, and community involvement should be developed and applied carefully and conscientiously. It behooves all involved in international educational exchange to assure adherence to these principles to enrich our institutions and benefit both U.S.-born and international students on our campuses.

As the world shrinks, borders are opened, and nations become more interdependent even as they gain individual independence, students must not only be internationally aware, they must be knowledgeable of issues beyond their cities, countries, and continents. The international dimension is critical to a well-conceived educational program. If U.S. higher education institutions admit qualified international students, communicate policies and procedures on English language proficiency and financial support clearly and concisely, and provide these students once they arrive on campus with the information, services, and resources they need to be successful, the ripple effect results will be well worth the care and concern given these important areas. The entire campus will reap the many rewards of having international students in our classrooms, laboratories, residence halls, and all the areas encompassed by student affairs.

References

Artman, R.B. (1986). Intercultural communications perspectives for residence hall staff. In R. Reiff (Ed.), *Living and learning for international interchange: A sourcebook for housing personnel* (pp. 3-10). Washington, D.C.: National Association for Foreign Student Affairs.

College Board, The. (1989). *Entering higher education in the United States: A guide to admissions and financial planning for students from other countries.* New York: author.

Elkins, R. (1989, December). Are international students important? *American Association of Collegiate Registrars and Admissions Officers Data Dispenser,* 9(4), 5.

Friedman, N. (1987). *Mentors and supervisors.* New York: Institute of International Education.

Goodwin, C.D., and Nacht, M. (1983). *Absence of decision.* New York: Institute of International Education.

Institute of International Education (1989). *Open doors 1988/89: Report on international educational exchange.* New York: author.

Limbird, M., and Owen, D. (1987). Create a positive climate for international recruitment on your campus. In S. MacGowan (Ed.), *The admissions strategist: Recruiting in the 1980s* (pp. 8-12). New York: The College Board.

National Association for Foreign Student Affairs (1978). *Selection and admission of foreign students.* Washington, D.C.: author.

National Association for Foreign Student Affairs (1979). *Standards and principles for professional staff and volunteers.* Washington, D.C.: author.

National Association for Foreign Student Affairs (1983). *Policy and practice in the administration of foreign student finances.* Washington, D.C.: author.

Peterson, M. (1987). What's the ticket to success in recruiting international students? In S. MacGowan (Ed.), *The admissions strategist: Recruiting in the 1980s* (pp. 1-4). New York: The College Board.

Quann, C.J., and Associates (1979). *Admissions, academic records, and registrar services.* San Francisco: Jossey-Bass Publisher, Inc.

Reiff, R.F. (Ed.). (1986). *Living and learning for international interchange: A sourcebook for housing personnel.* Washington, D.C.: National Association for Foreign Student Affairs.

Solmon, L.C., and Young, B.J. (1987). *The foreign student factor: Impact on American higher education.* New York: Institute of International Education.

Stern, L.; Tower, T.; and Doney, F. (1986). International housing. In R. Reiff (Ed.), *Living and learning for international interchange: A sourcebook for housing personnel* (p. 12). Washington, D.C.: National Association for Foreign Student Affairs.

CHAPTER SIX

Integrating Foreign Students into the University Community

Tom Thielen and Martin Limbird

The inclusion of international students in the myriad of leadership development and other campus programming activities has not been a primary focus of student affairs staff as annual programming plans are made. This condition can be partially explained by certain patterns among U.S. student affairs staff working with international students. On many U.S. campuses, international student services often resemble a doctor/patient, social service structure. By contrast, American students benefit from student affairs staff who offer leadership development training that leads to active involvement in the democratic process of self-governance. The failure to integrate international students into this aspect of campus life represents a missed critical "teaching-learning moment" for the entire educational community.

This chapter defines integration as "making whole or complete by adding or bringing together parts." In this context, it is asserted that American universities cannot be "whole or complete" without student affairs staff responsibly involving international students more fully in campus life.

RESEARCH ON INTERNATIONAL STUDENTS

Much has been written in the last 20 years on concerns and issues confronted by international students studying in the United States. Largely absent until recently has been discussion of how international students contribute to Americans' learning about other countries and cultures. Burn (1988) questions whether the mere presence of international students will contribute to the "internationalization" of a university, opening debate on what is the "right mix" of U.S. and international students on a campus. This debate has moved the question of how many international students a campus should enroll into a more critical domain. For example, what are our domestic students learning from having foreign classmates? Questions such as this may stimulate the following: To what extent are international students integrated into campus life? Can student affairs staff and faculty work together to set and achieve goals on this issue? Are student affairs professionals prepared to provide leadership to internationalizing the university through the integration of international students in campus life?

STUDENT AFFAIRS TRAINING
FROM AN INTERNATIONAL PERSPECTIVE

Today's student affairs staff are products of a curriculum that emphasizes our culture's peculiar view of student development. The U.S. system of higher education is hybrid in nature, borrowing major educational and organizational concepts from several European systems.

The driving concepts behind the student affairs movement in higher education originated, however, in this country. The importance of individual differences, of educating the "total person," and of out-of-class involvement as key parts of the student's total education are uniquely representative of American values. These principles have been the foundation for what is called the intentional intervention approach, the dominant thrust among student affairs professionals on American college campuses during the latter part of the 20th century.

The more than 10-fold growth since 1945 in the number of international students on U.S. campuses has created a more cosmopolitan student body in which to apply these indigenously inspired concepts. However, the increase in the number of international students has not resulted in out-of-class involvement of these students in more than extremely limited opportunities. The premise of this section is that such limitations exclude students from perhaps one of the unique dimensions of an educational sojourn in this country: the opportunity to fuse classroom learning with developmentally inspired leadership experiences that student affairs staff provide.

The curriculum in higher education masters and doctoral programs should include more awareness and sensitivity to the multicultural quality of U.S. campus populations and that planned intervention strategies be implemented to involve both international and American students. This implies enrichment of student personnel graduate programs with developmental learning approaches that can be used effectively with students from all parts of the world. As a first step, this inquiry should begin by recognizing that all parties involved have somewhat different motives for achieving integration of international students into U.S. campus life.

Motives for Integration

Three groups have a stake in the extent of integrating international students into campus life: student affairs staff who coordinate such services; the institution, in terms of its interest in international education; and the international students. Within each group are gaps between what is stated as motives for integration and what the actual practices are. An analysis of these varied motives is essential to understanding this issue.

As suggested earlier, the thrust of campus services to international students traditionally has focused on survival skills at initial orientation rather than developmental skills enrichment. To this extent, an international student services office resembles more a hospital emergency room than a wellness clinic. This medical metaphor becomes more appropriate when contrasting the operational activities of international student services staff and personnel working with American students.

Leadership skills development in theory and practice are the mainstay of support services for American residence hall and student organization officers, preparing them to plan, conduct, and evaluate activities effectively. By contrast, student affairs staff seem to insulate international students from unfamiliar social patterns. Such practices, while well meaning, do not provide the social tools and skills necessary for becoming involved in American campus life.

Research on this topic at Iowa State University analyzed international students' attitudes about the range of services provided them by their advisers, dating from the students' arrival on campus until they achieved alumni status (Fystrom & Peterson, 1980). This study determined that respondents recommended more emphasis be placed on skills development to become involved in campus life and to prepare for practical work experience prior to returning home. These findings challenged the efforts of staff whose motives were more protective than developmental and thus led to needed shifts in staff priorities.

The changing nature of institutional interests in international education is effectively summarized in *Abroad & Beyond* (Goodwin & Nacht, 1988), wherein promotion of international study is believed to be the "wave" that progressive institutions will ride throughout the 1990s. Regrettably, many such institutions will fail to involve resident international students as resources in achieving this contemporary objective. Of more concern are the institutions whose recruitment brochures speak glowingly of international student services, but in fact, whose motive of recruiting abroad is largely based on economic considerations. Unfortunately, institutional motives for recruiting and integrating international students can be extremely volatile, changing dramatically as new chief academic officers or presidents are installed on some U.S. campuses.

The motives of international students themselves toward understanding and becoming involved in American life cannot be judged solely by their essays that accompany their applications for admission. Limbird (1990) observed in his study of Koreans educated in the United States that recent graduates placed less value on involvement with Americans and other nationalities than did those who sought to be hired by major Korean conglomerates and trading companies. These firms' goals were clear: to hire those students who could communicate effectively and work with people of different cultures.

Increasing their chances for employment in the home country could be a strong motive for international students to integrate into U.S. campus life. For many Korean students, participation in student groups prior to U.S. study is commonplace. Their relative lack of experience with democratic institutions in these Korean student groups makes involvement in U.S. student development activities a particularly valuable tool for many Koreans studying in this country.

There are, however, instances where some international students are motivated to avoid contact with Americans, fearing they could be influenced by values that are not appreciated in their home cultures. An example of this isolating mode is evidenced among the students and scholars from China whose commitment to democratic principles were dealt a tragic blow in Tiananmen Square in June 1989. Even if today's students from China are reluctant to be openly involved in U.S. campus life, consider the benefits offered American student leaders who explore effective leadership styles across cultures with their fellow students from China. Dialogue between international and American students on meaningful cross-cultural issues makes the university experience the universal experience it should be. Yet help is needed from student affairs staff to clarify student motives to make the integration of leadership development the norm rather than the exception. No other institutional professionals are better equipped to achieve integration as defined in this chapter.

METHODS FOR ACHIEVING INTEGRATION

A case has been made that student affairs staff are the best qualified through leadership skills development in integrating international and American students. If this effort is to be effective, faculty support and participation are essential as well. To illustrate this point, imagine two streams feeding into a river. The streams (representing various ethnic and cultural groups) flow separately within the river's boundaries (the curriculum and the independently determined student development strategy), coexisting during the years of study, but interrelating almost not at all. The result is that the richness of a diverse student body is not shared and delays the merging that will occur ultimately as the waters of both streams join in the ocean, or when all graduates enter the same world of work and citizenship.

Imagine further the river's banks intentionally altered by student affairs staff and faculty who realize the advantages of their own interaction during the college years. The curriculum or banks have been expanded and contracted to create both eddies and rapids through which the students are obliged to use their education in light of the realities of their interconnectedness in the world. Such changes in the river's path can occur when faculty and student affairs staff recognize that they must begin to more closely interrelate their respective experiences and interventions into the educational process.

The metaphor of the river used to describe the ideal university learning environment creates an even more compelling message when one views the potential lost from not intentionally involving international and American students together in practical activities and experiences within a meaningful and understood theoretical framework. The increasing importance of understanding as well as implementing democratic principles worldwide gives credence to faculty and student affairs staff collaborating on meaningful integration experiences.

The results of planned interaction can and do contribute to classroom instruction of global issues, as well as in cocurricular skills development. Mestenhauser's (1976) *Learning with Foreign Students* remains an excellent example of how student affairs staff and faculty can collaborate to involve international students willingly as educational resources for the benefit of all students. Mestenhauser (1976) defines learning objectives that a typical instructor in international studies may wish to develop and that a typical foreign student could use to obtain "practical, integrative and relevant experiences" (p. 7).

Christensen and Thielen (1983) emphasize the need to go beyond traditional boundaries when involving the university community in cross-cultural activities. They maintain that faculty with overseas experience as Peace Corps volunteers or former Fulbright grantees are often among the most willing to integrate an international student into classroom instruction. Other potential cooperating faculty might include those who are adoptive parents, host family members for international students, former study abroad program leaders, foreign service or overseas military personnel, or parents of study abroad participants. Obtaining volunteers through the above methods increases the diversity of academic disciplines involved beyond the traditional social science disciplines.

Given the acumen of student affairs staff members in group dynamics and development, it would be natural for them to be prime instigators in inviting a new constituency to form around the goal of integrating international students into the campus. Involving international students in this catalytic role can establish a democratically generated interest group. The importance of this type of enterprise is that it helps validate the student affairs staff's skills in affecting the way learning about the world occurs on campus.

Faculty can also encourage their advisees from other countries to take part in such activities by awarding them academic credit. While giving credit for the learning that occurs from such activities rarely is the prime incentive for taking part, it does attach a standard measure to the activity. Grading such integration activities is useful principally in fitting the experiential learning into the broader framework of the total educational experience. Mestenhauser (1976) cites this same activity as an incentive for involving

American students in interviews with international students as part of a class project.

One cautionary note important to involving international students as classroom resource persons is that it is inappropriate to cast them as "experts" in all matters pertaining to their home countries. It is appropriate to pose questions indirectly such as, "What are the opinions of students/people your age/government officers about the issue of _____?" Few people are comfortable with questions that cast their country or culture in a poor light; hence, such questions are to be avoided or are to be used only after a level of trust has been established in the class.

MEASURING INTEGRATION

The impact of many educational efforts by student affairs staff is lost because it is not subjected to rigorous research. Applying responsible research techniques to the process and outcome of integration holds great promise for the entire educational community.

At the descriptive level, while much has been recommended in terms of integrating international students, little has been published which describes the process of faculty/staff/international student bonding that occurs. At a more rigorous level, variable treatments of intercultural exposure invite experimental design analysis in such areas as the involvement of international students as cultural resource persons in class. On a longitudinal level, the impact of interacting with international students creates lifelong personal ties in this increasingly mobile global society. Research needs to be done on the extent to which this exposure has influenced careers, attitudes, or concerns of the graduate 5, 15, or 25 years after leaving the institution.

Measuring integration can also be done by retaining promising faculty as well as interculturally curious students. Specifically, a campus that celebrates the diversity of its community describes itself as having a more appealing climate than one that ignores its intercultural learning potential. As a result, institutions actively making the most of integrating international students reflect a desired quality to some junior faculty who seek a cosmopolitan environment in which to live and work. This same appeal extends to the promising future undergraduate who has studied foreign languages, perhaps been a part of a family that has traveled abroad, or hosted a high school exchange student. By analyzing why students choose a particular undergraduate college, the chance to know and interact with international students may be a powerful recruiting tool for the globally conscious high school graduate.

The examples above indicate the potential value of short- and long-range measurement of the impact of international student integration. This is a fertile area for valuable applied research if promoted by the student affairs staff as instigator. The authors' experiences indicate that there are faculty who will enthusiastically add their creative thinking and research skills to investigate the questions central to the cultural integration theme. An important outcome of this collaboration beyond the knowledge is the natural linking of colleagues from the curricular and noncurricular segments of the university. This linkage not only provides knowledge on the importance of community, but also provides the laboratory for community involvement.

DEVELOPING A FRAMEWORK
FOR RESEARCH

A key initial step in legitimizing integration into institutional priorities may well be overcoming concern about the quality of research on international students. This point is borne out by Spaulding and Flack's (1976) work in which they describe research concerning international students in the United States as being methodologically uneven, conceptually and theoretically unfocused, topically wide ranging but seldom interrelated (p. 275). Therefore, it is in the interest of each campus with integration activities to establish parameters on the projects undertaken and studied for research purposes.

Table 1 presents such a framework, developed under the direction of Clubine (1978) at Iowa State University. Clubine (1978) believes that such a framework would guide faculty supervising research on international education issues toward producing a comprehensive institution-wide data base useful to the entire university. His goal is to reduce the proliferation of unfocused, nonintegrated studies on international students.

Table 1

Research Parameters for Studies on International Students and Scholars

I. Studies Based on Admissions Data
(studies of data which may predict success)

° TOEFL scores
° Standardized test data: MSAT, ACT, SAT, GRE
° Academic achievement in university attended previous to study in the United States

° Sources and amounts of financial support

II. Studies of Academic Progress
(rate of progress; relevance of curricula)

° Length of study
° Flexibility of curriculum
° Relationship of curricular content to situations in home
culture
° Level of academic achievement
° Amount and level of participation in academic department
and chosen professional field

III. Adjustment, Evaluation, and Impact Studies
(studies of early- and long-term adjustment and satisfaction)

° The impact of orientation programs
° Academic achievement the first two quarters and its
relationship to longer-range achievement
° The interaction of relationships with U.S. students, faculty,
and community members and adjustment
° The effect of the students' involvement with their own
cultures
° Studies of international families

IV. Studies of Faculty Members
(relative to attitudes, perception, evaluation of students,
flexibility, program opportunities)

° Departmental attitudes and admission policies
° Attitudes toward international education
° Studies of advising systems
° Studies of thesis supervision

V. Context Studies
(studies of attitudes of U.S. persons toward international
students)

° Faculty and staff attitudes
° U.S. students' attitudes
° Community members' attitudes
° Communication media attitudes
° The effects of U.S. persons' attitudes on international students
° Global changes and issues and their impacts on U.S. attitudes

VI. Demographic Studies
(analysis of data describing the international student group)
° Census of persons
° Patterns of enrollments and their shifts
° Identification and analysis of international persons data such as number of graduate and undergraduate students, postdoctoral persons, and faculty members
° Employment status of students
° Types of visas held

VII. Financial Studies
(costs and benefits of international student education and sources of financial support)
° Cost to the student of attending the university
° Amount and sources of student support
° Cost of specialized services for international students
° Costs of thesis and dissertation research
° Financial contributions of international students to the local and state economies

VIII. Follow-up Studies
(studies of former students one, five, and ten years after they have graduated or left ISU)
° Initial position back home and relationship to education received in the United States
° Evaluation by students of their total U.S. experience
° Study progress by alumni in their occupation or profession

INTEGRATION IN AN INSTITUTIONAL CONTEXT

The thrust of this chapter has been to view integration of international students as a means to an end — that is, to increase collaboration of faculty and staff in student development-inspired learning, specifically increasing the prospect for intercultural learning on campus for all. This is, however, but one of many "vehicles to internationalization" (Harari, 1989), and the 12 options that Harari proposes for consideration are found in Table 2.

Table 2
Vehicles to Internationalization

1. The infusion of disciplines with international content
2. Comparative approaches
3. Issue-oriented approaches and interdisciplinary studies
4. Area studies and civilizational approaches
5. International studies and intercultural studies
6. International development (theory and practice)
7. The role of foreign languages as an integral part of the internationalization of undergraduate education
8. The internationalization of preprofessional studies and professional schools
9. Faculty and staff development and research in the international area
10. Institutional linkages and global networking of scholars
11. The involvement of U.S. students who have studied abroad and international students in the international enrichment of the curriculum and the campus
12. The involvement of students and faculty in internships, research, and other opportunities in internationally oriented business firms and other appropriate agencies at home or abroad

From the above, it is clear that international/American student interaction is but one aspect of capturing an institution-wide focus on how to learn about the world. To his credit, Harari (1989) departs significantly from others writing in this field in terms of how he views the contribution of international students to the overall U.S. educational enterprise. Rather than seeing them as a group to be simply tolerated within academe, Harari (1989) urges their involvement to overcome the "absence of mutual reinforcement (which) often exists between the curriculum and the myriads of activities in which an institution might involve itself in the local community and overseas" (p. 1). These insights clearly reinforce the objectives of the authors in the larger context of internationalizing the university.

CONCLUSION

Thus, the integration of international and U.S. students provides an opportunity to relate student development expertise to the curriculum. Planned interventions will assist student affairs staff to facilitate the bridging of the academic curriculum with out-of-class activities in developing leadership skills in a cross-cultural context. As the 1990s progress and the old geopolitical barriers that have divided nations for decades fall, leaders in American higher education must be inventive in assuring that the university years make the most of the opportunities available to bring together international and American students. Returning to the metaphor of the river, a poem about friendship seems appropriate:

I would like to think of our friendship
as being like that of two rivers, which
one day, within the fleeting moments of time,
met and suffused — two rivers that arose from

different valleys to flow together to the sea.
As time would have it, our lives, like rivers,
stir and break to curve separate courses
toward destiny's distant, alas, uncharted waters.
No longer will the rivers together flow.
Time and space will be between them.
But as friends who together flowed
through the valley of knowledge
each will retain a part of the other.
Sometimes rivers meet again, if only for a span,
so perhaps somewhere within the eternity of time
our lives again will converge. But . . .
if even for a moment, we can relive together
the friendship we have had, I will cherish until death
the mere fact that I have known you.

— author unknown

Regrettably, the American academic experience has never reached its full potential for different cultures to learn with and from each other, as the above poem suggests. There are too many barriers for this learning to take place without planned intervention. The challenge to the reader is first believe in the necessity of integration of cultures and then develop strategies to intrude on the patterns of the institution. Integration becomes realistic when the academic community is challenged to appreciate differences and celebrate similarities between and among cultures.

References

Burn, B.B. (1988). International exchange and curricular change. *Phi Kappa Phi Journal*, Fall, 31-34.

Christensen, G.C., and Thielen, T.B. (1983). Cross-cultural activities: Maximizing benefits. In H.M. Jenkins and Associates, *Educating students from other nations* (pp. 210-36). San Francisco: Jossey-Bass Publisher, Inc.

Clubine, E. (1978). Memo to administration at Iowa State University.

Fystrom, L., and Peterson, D. (1980). *A case study*. Ames, Iowa: Iowa State University.

Goodwin, C.D., and Nacht, M. (1988). *Abroad & beyond*. Cambridge: Cambridge University Press.

Harari, M. (1989). *Internationalization of higher education: Effecting institutional change in the curriculum and campus ethos*. Long Beach, CA: Center for International Education, California State University.

Limbird, M. (1990). *The American experience in retrospect: Views of U.S. educated Koreans inside Korean business conglomerates*. Washington, D.C.: National Association for Foreign Student Affairs.

Mestenhauser, J. (1976). *Learning with foreign students*. Minneapolis: University of Minnesota.

Spaulding, S., and Flack, M.J. (1976). *The world's students in the United States*. New York: Praeger Publishers.

CHAPTER SEVEN

Global Trends
In Overseas Study

William K. Cummings

The rate of global expansion in overseas study is sensitive to changes in the world economy. As Figure 1 illustrates, the rate of expansion was most rapid during the latter half of the 1960s and the latter half of the 1970s, two periods of relative health in the world economy. But expansion significantly slowed in the early 1970s, accompanying the post-Vietnam War recession, and in the early 1980s, a time when the economic growth of most of the advanced economies slowed.

Until the early 1980s, there was a steady increase in the number of students from all regions, as indicated in Table 1. Africa's overall numerical increase was most rapid, its share nearly doubled between 1963 and 1978. There is, however, much variation among African countries. Nigeria's expansion has been three times the overall African rate while there has been an absolute decline in the numbers from several other African nations.

Figure 1
Foreign Student Enrollment, 1954/55–1987/88

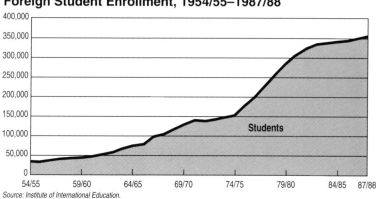

Source: Institute of International Education.

Since the early 1980s, the numbers from the Middle East and South America have decreased. While the figures are not available for all host countries, the United States reports a 33 percent decline between 1980-81 and 1984-85 in the number of international students from the Middle East, and more modest declines for the other regions.

By region, Asia currently supplies the largest proportion of international students (Cummings, 1989). Among the Asian subregions, South Asia's rate of growth peaked in the 1960s and the Middle East peaked in the early 1980s. Currently, the supply from Southeast Asia appears to be slowing while that from East Asia continues to increase at a modest rate. Among the ten countries supplying the most international students, over one-third have consistently been in Asia (Cummings, 1989). As illustrated in Table 2, in the 1970s Middle Eastern countries displaced Far Eastern countries as the largest suppliers. But by 1985, Asian countries were once again the largest suppliers in absolute terms.

However, when the population size of the Middle Eastern countries is taken into account, their propensity to supply students is even more impressive. Six of the ten countries in the world with the highest ratio of students

Table 1

Region of Origin of International Students

Region of Origin	1963 Number	%	1968 Number	%	1973 Number	%	1978 Number	%	1985 Number	%
Africa	35587	12.2	48067	11.8	90390	15.2	159662	19.3	169777	19.2
North America	39515	13.6	58999	14.5	77210	13.0	79652	9.6	69792	7.9
South America	21334	7.3	25194	6.2	26855	4.5	44457	5.4	35563	4.0
Asia	122356	42.3	182445	44.8	260713	43.9	371711	44.9	428764	48.5
Europe/Russia	68443	23.6	87919	21.6	130759	22.0	163569	19.8	177089	20.0
Oceania	2880	1.0	4362	1.1	7393	1.2	8001	1.0	7910	.9
Total of Known Origin	290615	100.0	406986	100.0	593320	100.0	827052	100.0	883895	100.0
Origin Not Specified	8919		21879		44210		15653		54909	
Grand Total	299534		28865		37530		842705		938804	

Source: UNESCO

Figure 2
Foreign Students by World Region of Origin, 1954/55–1987/88

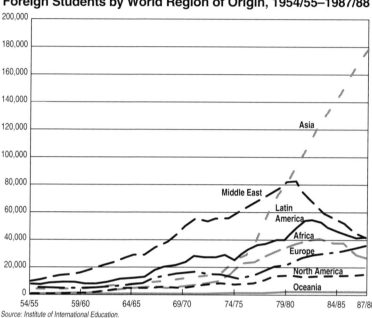

Source: Institute of International Education.

exported to population are in the Middle East (Cummings, 1989).

The major direction of international student flow is from the developing countries to the developed countries. Indeed, in 1980, as indicated in Table 3, over two-thirds of all international students were in only five advanced societies.

Table 3 shows that among the advanced societies, the United States' share of international students has steadily increased. Currently, it receives over one-third of all international students. In recent years, France has retained its share, while the United Kingdom and Germany are slipping. In the case of the United Kingdom, since 1978 there has been a sharp decline not only in the proportional share of the global total but also in the absolute number of international students. Japan is still far behind the other

Table 2

The Ten Countries Supplying the Largest Number of International Students in 1968, 1980 and 1985

1968		1980		1985	
China	21522	Iran	58204	China	53378
USA	20489	Malaysia	32850	Malaysia	38980
Canada	15061	Greece	30597	Iran	37054
Syria	12121	China	27055	Greece	34267
UK	10480	Nigeria	23715	Morocco	29683
West Germany	10077	Morocco	20981	Korea	25978
Greece	9784	USA	19692	Jordan	24410
South Korea	9283	Hong Kong	19646	Hong Kong	24293
Italy	8962	West Germany	16894	West Germany	23114
Malaysia	7582	Jordan	15833	USA	20614
				India	20389
				Japan	17926
				Canada	17205
				Italy	17004
				Nigeria	16549
				Syria	16423

Source: UNESCO Statistical Yearbook

Table 3
The Ten Countries Receiving the Largest Numbers of International Students

	1968			1980			1985	
Country	Number	% of Total Overseas Students	Country	Number	% of Total Overseas Students	Country	Number	% of Total Overseas Students
USA	121362	28.3	USA	311882	33.9	USA	349620	37.2
France	36300	8.5	France	110763	12.0	France	126762	13.5
W. Germany	26783	6.2	Russia	62942	6.9	W. Germany	79354	8.5
Lebanon	18811	4.4	W. Germany	61841	6.7	UK	48686	5.2
Canada	17414	4.1	UK	56003	6.1	Italy	28068	3.0
UK	16154	3.3	Lebanon	31018	3.4	Canada	27210	2.9
Russia	16100	3.9	Canada	29443	3.1	Lebanon	25515	2.7
Egypt	14008	3.3	Italy	27784	3.0	Belgium	20095	2.1
Argentina	7103	1.7	Egypt	21751	2.4	Saudi Arabia	17970	1.9
Italy	7103	1.7	Romania	15998	1.3	Australia	16075	1.7

Source: UNESCO Statistical Yearbook

advanced societies in receiving international students, but the numbers going there are increasing rapidly.

Several developing countries are also hosts to large numbers of international students. Table 3 above indicates for 1985 that Lebanon and Saudi Arabia were among the world's top ten receivers of international students; to this list could be added the Syrian Arab Republic which was 14th with 12,909 incoming students and Egypt which was 15th with 12,235. Brazil, India, and the Philippines also receive large numbers. It is likely that the numbers in most of these developing countries will continue to increase.

The great majority of international students are self-supporting. While comprehensive data are not available, Table 4 indicates the proportions relying on different types of support while studying in the United States and Japan. Students from developing countries tend to specialize in science and engineering. In contrast, those from the developed societies tend to specialize in the humanities and arts, especially when they study in developing societies.

Student's choice of study evidences considerable sensitivity to leading-edge trends in the global economy. In the early 1970s, engineering was the growth area. In the late 1970s, the numbers of international students entering business and management programs increased sharply. Currently, as illustrated in Table 5 with U.S. data, the hot field is mathematics and computer science.

At least among international students coming to the United States, as illustrated in Table 6, the proportion of international students selecting undergraduate, graduate, and other levels of study has been remarkably constant over time. However, in the United Kingdom, there has been a trend toward an increase in the proportion selecting graduate-level studies.

Countries differ widely in the proportion they send for different levels of study. Further, over time the proportion

Table 4
Primary Source of Funds of International Students
in the United States and Japan

Primary Source of Funds	US 1984	Japan 1983
Institutional:		
Host Government	2.1%	20.0%
Host Country Private Sponsor	1.9%	ND
Host Country College or		
University	11.6%	ND
Home Country Government	12.0%	ND
Foreign Private Sponsor	2.9%	ND
Other Institutional Sources	3.9%	ND
Personal and Family	66.2%	ND

Source: Institute of International Education

from particular countries at different degree levels may significantly shift. For example, the proportion from Taiwan seeking graduate study in the United States has steadily increased from 47 percent in 1954 to 80 percent in 1987, whereas the proportion from Japan seeking graduate study has steadily declined from 53 percent in 1959 to 29 percent in 1987.

HOW DOES THE FLOW
DIFFER BY COUNTRY?

In this author's view, countries from which international students come seem to fall into three groups:

Table 5
Distribution of International Students in the USA
By Field of Study, 1987

	Number	% Change From 1979
Engineering	73,880	− 9.4
Business & Management	66,990	+ 42.0
Mathematics & Computer Science	35,400	+130.0
Physical & Life Sciences	29,250	+ 33.7
Social Sciences	27,650	+ 22.7
Fine & Applied Arts	15,860	+ 10.5
Humanities	14,250	+ 25.7
Intensive English Language	14,030	+ 15.3
Health Sciences	13,910	+ 27.0
Education	11,140	− 9.7
Agriculture	7,930	− 9.4
Other	25,100	+ 99.0
Undeclared	20,790	+ 3.0
TOTAL	356,190	+ 24.4

Source: Institute of International Education

■ Early Development. Countries such as Indonesia and Malaysia have relatively elite higher educational systems and/or these systems do not offer equal opportunity to the members of all the indigenous groups. For this reason, large numbers of students seek either short-cycle or first-degree programs in development-related fields such as business, computers, and engineering.

Table 6
Distribution of Academic Level for International Students in the USA
Selected Years: 1963/64 to 1987/88

| Academic Year | Academic Level | | | All Levels |
	Under-graduate	Graduate	Other	
1963/64	48.2	41.9	9.9	100.0
1969/70	47.2	45.3	7.3	100.0
1973/74	50.4	44.3	5.3	100.0
1979/80	58.1	36.2	5.7	100.0
1981/82	59.5	35.5	5.0	100.0
1983/84	57.9	52.9	3.9	100.0
1984/85	57.8	35.8	6.6	100.0
1985/86	54.6	38.5	6.9	100.0
1986/87	51.8	41.8	6.4	100.0
1987/88	49.6	43.9	6.5	100.0

Source: Institute of International Education

■ Late Development. Countries that have made greater strides in developing an indigenous higher educational system nevertheless look to overseas institutions for graduate-level programs appropriate for training their scholars and researchers; many of these students pursue disciplines that are thought to contribute to development.

■ Developed. In Asia, Japan is the only highly developed country and the majority of the Japanese students who go overseas enter first-degree programs, usually in the humanities and social sciences and often for only a year. Compared to most other Asian societies, women are a large portion of the Japanese international students. Many of them specialize in English as a foreign language, the fine arts, or related fields.

Depending on which of these patterns is most characteristic of a country, we can see that its students' objectives and hence the program composition will vary.

VARIABLES FOR COUNTRY DIFFERENCES IN FLOW

In most cases, the decision to go overseas, including the search for information and finances, is largely personal (Cummings, 1984). But this decision is shaped by the national context of each student. Thus, it is appropriate to look at country-level variables when accounting for flows.

A considerable amount of insight has been developed over the past several years concerning the determinants of student flows. The determinants of the flow are best thought of in terms of two distinctive processes, as depicted in the upper and lower halves of Figure 3: First, the factors that influence national differences in the likelihood of going overseas; and second, the factors affecting the likelihood that students from a given country will select a U.S. institution for their study.

Why Do Countries Differ in Their Likelihood of Sending Students Overseas?

The following national characteristics have been shown to be related to the likelihood of a nation sending proportionately large numbers of students overseas (Cummings, 1984).

■ Basic Human Resource Capacity. If a national education system provides large numbers of young people with the basic qualifications for study at the college level, more young people from that nation will consider overseas study.

The tendency to go overseas, however, may be offset by the availability of a large number of domestic places. For example, the United States and Japan, which have the world's highest college-level enrollment rates, send few students overseas relative to their population size. The large number of Malaysian international students occurs in part because of the shortage of domestic higher education places, especially for the academically able Chinese minority.

In Korea and other Asian countries, higher educational systems have undergone rapid expansion in recent years, but this has not significantly affected the propensity of going overseas. There are three ready explanations for this seeming anomaly:

° domestic higher educational expansion reflects a large and unmet private demand that is only partially accommodated by the increase in domestic places
° to staff the newly created domestic institutions, a new pool of scholars with training at the graduate level is required
° the rapid quantitative expansion of domestic higher education is usually not accompanied by qualitative upgrading, thus enhancing the attraction of international education both for undergraduate and especially for graduate-level programs.

■ Domestic Scarcity of Science and Technology. Because much of the demand for international study focuses on the scientific and technical fields, the extent to which the domestic system provides opportunities in these areas may curtail the tendency to go overseas. Singapore, whose educational system places relatively more stress on these fields at both secondary and postsecondary levels, sends fewer students than Hong Kong, where the higher education system focuses on the humanities.

■ Linguistic Isolation. Nations that conduct their education in the same languages as the leading receiver nations are likely to send more students than do nations which use local languages as the medium of instruction. Thus Southeast Asia, Hong Kong, and Singapore, which rely on English as the main language of instruction, send more students relative to their population than countries such as Thailand and Indonesia. Of course, in many countries which rely on an indigenous language as the primary medium of instruction, metropolitan languages tend to be introduced at the secondary level, thus providing students with the rudimentary language skills necessary for studying overseas.

■ Financial Capacity. Nations with higher standards of living will send relatively more students than poorer nations. In the more affluent nations, greater numbers of families are likely to have the resources to cover the considerable expenses associated with overseas study. Similarly, governments are likely to have larger revenues, and hence more funds available to finance overseas study. It is partly because of their recent economic success that the Middle East nations have begun to send large numbers of students overseas.

■ Economic Volatility. Regardless of a nation's standard of living, in times of rapid economic growth the number of students going overseas is likely to increase; and in periods of recession the numbers decrease. Thus in recent years, as oil prices have declined, nations whose economies are highly dependent on oil revenues have been sending fewer students overseas.

■ Domestic Opportunities for Higher Education. Students in large countries can choose from a wide variety of domestic higher educational opportunities while those from small countries, having fewer domestic opportunities, are more likely to consider foreign study. For example, in Asia relatively larger proportions of Taiwanese and Sri Lankan students go overseas compared to mainland Chinese and Indian students.

■ Economic Interdependence. If a national economy is dependent on international transactions, the young people of that nation will see their careers linked with the actions of multinational corporations and foreign economic centers. In part to learn more about these external centers of action, many of these young people will seek to study overseas. It is partly for this reason that the sending rates of Hong Kong and Singapore are high compared to other Asian countries. The direction of student flow is likely to overlap with the direction of the international transactions; while these countries were once closely linked to the United Kingdom and their students went primarily to the United Kingdom, today they have closer ties with the United States.

■ Facilitating Institutions. With the cumulative experience of a country sending students overseas, the practice becomes institutionalized. Young people in the secondary schools and universities spend much of their time discussing overseas study options. Profit-making firms are established to facilitate the search of those interested in overseas study. In the case of advanced societies, reciprocal study abroad programs are negotiated. With the institutionalization of overseas study, a country's tendency to send students overseas is likely to stabilize, even if other conditions alter.

■ Ethnic Disadvantages. In nations with enduring ethnic or racial tensions, there will be an especially strong tendency for minority group members to seek overseas study. For example, in Malaysia and Indonesia, members of the minority Chinese group are especially likely to seek overseas study at their own expense. In contrast, in Singapore, members of the minority Indian group are most likely to go overseas for study. In Sri Lanka, the Tamils view overseas study as a means to seek external opportunities.

■ Political Uncertainty. Nations experiencing political uncertainty are also likely to send large numbers of students overseas. With the announcement that Hong Kong would be reverting to mainland China in 1997, the numbers from Hong Kong seeking overseas study quickly increased. Similarly, the continuing political uncertainty in Korea, Taiwan, and the Philippines is a contributory factor in the overseas study decisions of young people in these countries.

Where Do International Students Go?

A parallel issue is the national destination international students select. As noted earlier, currently one-third of all international students are in the United States and an additional one-third are in the leading European countries of France, Germany, and the United Kingdom. The United States is the primary destination for Asian countries. But among Asian countries, the proportion sent to the United States varies. What factors influence these international patterns of student flow?

In the past, national ties following from the colonial era were an important factor influencing international student flow (Cummings & So, 1985). These continue to influence decisions, as illustrated by the preference of several of France's former African colonies to concentrate on France, and a continuing bias in certain of Britain's former colonies toward an education in the United Kingdom. But in most instances, these colonial ties seem to have become subordinated to other linkages. Specifically,

■ Cold-war related linkages have redirected national patterns of flow. The shift of the national flows of such nations as Korea, Taiwan, India, Thailand, Vietnam, Iran, and Egypt to the United States can be dated to the period when each of these nations received large amounts of technical and military assistance from the United States. Similarly, the large numbers of Indonesians going to Germany is a byproduct of extensive German technical assistance to that country.

■ The volume of economic exchange between nations also influences the direction of student flow. The rapid step-up in U.S. economic involvement in Southeast Asia from the early 1950s helps account for the shift in the student flow there from Europe to the United States. Currently, Japanese economic involvement in the region is resulting in increased student flow to Japan.

■ When nationals from a particular country take up residence and citizenship in a host country, this is likely to enhance the flow of students between the two countries. Especially since 1965, following the change in the U.S. immigration laws, large numbers of Asians have settled in the United States. Prior to 1965, the majority of Americans of Asian origin had come from East Asia; the new Asians are as likely to come from Southeast and South Central Asia. It is partly due to the information Asian Americans have supplied and the financial assistance they have provided that their countrymen and -women have selected the United States as a destination for overseas study.

■ Cultural linkages also facilitate the flow between national systems. As English has increasingly become recognized as the international language, it has come to be emphasized as the second language in educational systems around the world. The English language familiarity has directed students to host countries such as the United States, the United Kingdom, Canada, Australia, New Zealand, and India where English is the language of instruction.

■ The absorptive capacity of host country educational systems is also an important factor. In the European societies, by the mid 1970s, international students were taking up 5-10 percent of all places in higher education, causing domestic educators to question the advisability of further admissions. In contrast, in the vast American system international students constituted less than 3 percent and overall have caused little burden.

Indeed, it could be argued that the influx of Asian students has provided important assistance in at least some sectors of American higher education. From the mid 1970s, the U.S. domestic demand for science and engineering education declined. It was at this very time that the foreign demand in these specialties increased. The Asian students prevented the closing or shrinking of many of the departments in these fields. This convenient complementarity of supply and demand was not as evident in the European systems.

■ The great diversity of institutions in the American system accommodates students with varying levels of preparation and motivation. Weak students can be accepted in junior colleges where they acquire the remedial skills necessary for participation in more competitive sectors of higher education. Students with minimal English skills can improve their language skills in the numerous English as foreign language centers. Flexible admissions policies which enable students to come throughout the calendar year are another distinctive feature of the American system relative to the European alternatives.

■ Financial considerations also play an important role in student choice. The United Kingdom's decision to charge full-cost fees to international students led to a sharp decline in the number of students seeking education in Britain. Higher education in the United States is not inexpensive, but international students often discover opportunities for financial assistance or for part-time work on or off campus, thus enabling them to cover a substantial portion of their expenses.

RECENT CHANGES AND LOOKING AHEAD

Over the postwar period, this author has observed that the phenomenon of going overseas for study has become widely institutionalized in Asia. All governments have official agencies to supervise at least a part of the outflow, and in most countries numerous private entrepreneurs have established firms to assist students who wish to go overseas for study. On the receiving side, organizations such as the Institute of International Education and the British Council as well as international student services offices of particular universities have been established to provide services to facilitate international students.

With the extensive institutionalization of overseas study, this author has also noticed that the overseas experience increasingly becomes an extension of domestic study as much as an alternative. The nations with the largest domestic higher educational systems also send the largest numbers of students overseas; and, in most cases, as the domestic systems have expanded the volume going overseas has also increased (Cummings & So, 1985). For example, in the case of Korea, following the government's

1982 declaration of its intent to double the number of domestic higher educational places, the number of students going overseas sharply increased.

In the 1970s, many small countries with weak or restricted higher educational systems had exceptionally high sending rates and were also leading the list of top senders. These small countries continue to send large numbers, but it may be that they have reached the limits of their capacity to export students, at least to the advanced countries. Meanwhile, several much larger countries which have had relatively low sending rates have begun to increase their sending rates and to steadily expand the number of students they are sending overseas (Cummings, 1989).

These larger countries still have an enormous reserve of human resource capacity, so there is no way of judging what will be the future volume of their student export. But it is safe to say that these countries are capable of further expansion.

In the late 1970s, population size had a negligible relation with several of the flow indicators, but by 1987 it had a strong positive relation with the total volume sent to the United States and with the long-term growth in that volume. The large countries which have shown gains over the last decade include China, India, Pakistan, Korea, and Japan. Indonesia's volume to the United States, while evidencing a short-term decline in 1986-87, has also increased substantially over the past decade (Cummings, 1989).

Financial capacity is also an important factor in the ability of nations to send students overseas. In the late '70s, the financial capability of Middle Eastern nations suddenly improved due to the OPEC-engineered increase in oil revenues; a useful indicator of this change was the short-run improvement in the per capita GNP of these nations. With this sudden economic improvement, many of these nations sharply increased the rates and volume of their overseas sending. But by the early '80s, the OPEC advantage had weakened, and the level of sending from these countries also sagged.

In contrast with the short-run blip in the financial capacity of the OPEC nations has been the steady growth over the past two decades in the financial capacity of most Asian nations. In global terms, the Asian region has enjoyed the most continuous and rapid long-term economic growth of all the major regions (World Bank, 1987). The newly industrialized nations of Korea, Taiwan, Hong Kong, and Singapore lead this trend, followed by Japan (steady growth but a slower average rate), Malaysia, Thailand, and China. India, Pakistan, and Indonesia have also experienced moderate long-term growth in per capita GNP. Many nations in Africa and Latin America and several in the Middle East have experienced negligible to negative growth over the same period. Whereas in the '70s, GNP per capita had a strong correlation with sending rates and absolute volume, by the mid '80s, average growth in GNP per capita from 1965-86 was more strongly associated with overseas sending (Cummings, 1989).

Another observation has been that the relative value of currencies also influences financial capability. The currencies of Asia's leading export-oriented economies have over the '80s been under strong pressure to revalue relative to the dollar. The sharp jump in the value of the yen between 1986 (250 yen to the dollar) and 1987 (130 yen to the dollar) has made U.S. higher education much more attractive to Japanese consumers, and thus during 1986-88 the number of Japanese students coming to the United States experienced the sharpest increase since the early 1950s. The currencies of Korea and Singapore have already experienced modest appreciation, and will no doubt be under pressure for further appreciation over the next several years. As those currencies strengthen, the national purchasing power for U.S. higher education will correspondingly improve.

This analysis thus far has focused on variations between Asian nations. If we consider Asia as a whole, we can appreciate that the expansion of the Asian student flow builds on two fundamental characteristics of the Asian region: large populations and stable economic growth. These fundamentals are unlikely to change for the foreseeable future. Sixty percent of the world's population lives in Asia, and while the population growth rate in Asia (averaged 2.2 percent from 1965-85) is less than that for Africa (2.9 percent), Latin America (2.5 percent), or the Middle East (2.4 percent), the absolute and relative size of Asia will remain impressive (World Bank, 1987, pp. 6-7). In terms of economic growth, most nations in Asia have passed the take-off point and have solid prospects for diversified development, providing the world economy progresses. No other developing region has such promising prospects. The political stability of Asia is less certain, though important progress has been made over the past decade toward reducing regional tension through the formation of the Association of Southeast Asian Nations (ASEAN) and the decrease in conflict along the Thai-Vietnamese and Pakistan-Afghanistan borders. Compared to other regions, Asia is conflict free. Because of these fundamentals, it is reasonable to anticipate a continuing expansion of the Asian appetite for overseas study.

For a variety of reasons, the Asian student flow has become increasingly directed to the United States. The United States and Japan are the cornerstones of a new Pacific Rim trade and cultural zone. Historically, large numbers of Asians have immigrated, and outside of the Asian region their most common destination has been the United States. While earlier migration was primarily from

East Asia, over the past two decades the United States has received a large number of immigrants from Southeast and South Central Asia, thus broadening the Pacific Rim links (Cummings & So, 1985). In terms of economic growth and trade volume, the Pacific Rim zone is more dynamic and far larger than that covered by the Atlantic community or the socialist bloc.

As Asian students consider going overseas, they have various options. By virtue of the new Pan-Pacific consciousness, Europe's salience has waned. Within Asia, the higher educational systems of Australia, Japan, and New Zealand are relatively open to Asian students. But none of these systems, not even Japan with its 2.5 million places, begins to equal the capacity of the American system which accommodates 12.5 million students. Moreover, the American system where classes are taught in English and which has such an extraordinary range of opportunities in terms of quality and program is more accessible than the alternatives. Thus, as the Asian export of international students increases, the United States is destined to receive ever larger numbers of Asian students.

The expansion of the Asian student flow points to a number of opportunities for American higher educational institutions: the development of new study abroad and collaborative programs, including the need to send more American students to study scientific and technical subjects in Asian institutions to balance the level of high-tech literacy; the expansion of intensive English language programs; and the continuing prospects for the recruitment of highly qualified Asian students. The flow of Asian students to the United States adds over $1 billion to the American economy (Cummings, 1989).

In the context of overall decline in the number of students enrolled in American higher education, a continuing expansion in the supply of international students should be welcomed by higher educational leaders. With international students making up only 2.8 percent of all students in American higher education, there is still room for absorbing many more international students. However, there are at least two areas where some caution is warranted: (1) International students, and especially those from Asia, may make up too large a proportion of the student body in certain departments at certain universities, thus depriving these international students and their American counterparts of the benefits of diversity which are usually sought through international student exchange. (2) Also, the current majority of Asian students has emerged due to a precipitous decline in the proportion of students from all other major world regions except Europe. In the case of Africa, the Middle East, Latin America, and Oceania, the absolute numbers of international students are down relative to the early '80s. Thus, with diversity as a goal of international education, there is a need to consider the implications of these contrary trends.

CONCLUSION

Overseas study, for a variety of reasons, is clearly an expanding phenomena that yields much benefit to most of the participants. The concern in this essay, along with surveying trends, has been to introduce and compare several indicators useful for a sensitive analysis of this phenomena. Much of the analysis has focused on Asian countries because these countries provide the major share of international students and because of the relative availability of data on Asian countries. However, the general principles outlined in this chapter seem equally applicable to other parts of the world.

Looking to the years ahead, it is possible to speculate on emerging global trends that may influence overseas study. On the sending side, the following are several examples. There is reason to expect Latin America to emerge from its decade of economic stagnation and international debt; to the extent Latin American economies improve, increasing numbers of students from that area may seek overseas study. Similarly, the economic conditions of several African countries are improving, and moreover global interest in providing technical assistance for Africa is mounting. An important component of this assistance will be the opportunities for overseas study provided to African students.

On the receiving side, one of the most dramatic developments is Japan's recent program to increase its share of international students 10-fold to 100,000 students by the year 2000. If Japan succeeds in this program, the world volume of overseas students will increase by nearly 10 percent.

Distinct from the number of students going overseas are the structural arrangements enabling their movements. The traditional pattern has been for students to apply as individuals to foreign institutions. With the increasing volume of interested students, several arrangements have emerged. The United States pioneered in the study abroad concept wherein American institutions set up facilities overseas to facilitate the movement of large numbers of their students into particular foreign settings. This same pattern is now being replicated by Japanese institutions (Chambers & Cummings, 1990).

Yet another trend is for institutions of major receiver countries to set up branch campuses in countries where large numbers of prospective students are known to be present. American institutions began this practice in Malaysia and now are replicating it in Japan (Chambers & Cummings, 1990). Thus, as the volume of overseas study increases, new institutional arrangements will emerge. These arrangements will tend to further institutionalize the practice of overseas study, ensuring its long-term expansion.

References

Chambers, G., and Cummings, W. (1990). *Profiting from education.* New York: Institute of International Education.

Cummings, W. (1984, May). Going overseas for higher education: The Asian experience. *Comparative Education Review,* 28, 241-57.

Cummings, W. (1989, March). Trends seen in the flow of Asian students to the United States. *NAFSA Newsletter,* 40,5, 1.

Cummings, W., and So, W. (1985). The preference of Asian overseas students for the United States: An examination of the context. *Higher Education,* 14, 403-23.

World Bank (1987). *Social indicators of development, 1987.* Washington, D.C.: author.

CHAPTER EIGHT

Student Affairs Professionals As International Educators

A Challenge for the Next Century

Patricia Willer

There is an ancient Chinese saying: "May you be blessed with the opportunity to live in interesting times." These are indeed interesting times, both in the world and on college and university campuses. Part of the challenge of these interesting times is for higher education professionals to prepare today's college students to meet the complex needs of the world.

Recent political events in the world have been tumultuous. Major political upheavals in Russia and Central Europe, massive demonstrations with devastating governmental reactions in China, U.S. political and military interventions in Latin America, and the unification of Western Europe have all had tremendous impact on world affairs. The war in the Persian Gulf brought the realities of the interdependence of the world to the forefront of the consciousness of many in the United States.

Foreign investment in the United States, the opening of free markets in the communist countries of Europe, the ever-growing problems of Third World debt, and the increasing development of transnational corporations all point to a merging of national economies into regional and world economies. At the same time, acid rain, the deforestation of rain forests, population pressures, air and water pollution, and waste disposal have increasingly become environmental issues to be dealt with not only on local, regional, and national levels but internationally as well.

The world in the 21st century will be marked as increasingly connected in almost every area: business, politics, science and technology, communications. To exist in isolation, as nations or as individuals, will not be possible. At an ever-increasing rate, colleges and universities are recognizing this interdependence and the need to accommodate it as critically important. That importance is being reflected in institutional priorities and commitments. In fact, the "internationalization of the university" has been discussed as one of the most significant challenges facing higher education in the 1990s.

Harari (1981) states in a report sponsored by the American Association of State Colleges and Universities,

> The national and international policies and strategies pursued in the next two or three decades are complex. They no longer require the technical skills of only a few in each nation. They require the global literacy and global awareness of the populations around the world. International understanding has come to represent a very practical and urgent need, and clearly higher education has the major responsibility in this area in the long term (pp. 1-2).

The trend toward emphasizing the importance of international education was also reflected in a report from the Southern Governors' Association (1986) in which international education was identified as the single most important strategy to re-establish American leadership and competitiveness. Not unrelated is the recent study commissioned by the American Council on Education focusing on international studies and the American undergraduate in which higher education leaders were called upon to make a new commitment to provide international education to American undergraduates (Lambert, 1989).

But what does internationalization mean? It means providing a global perspective and expanded world view to every aspect of education for both students and faculty. It includes incorporating international content, materials, activities, and understandings into the teaching, research, and public service functions of the academy in response to this increasingly interdependent world. It provides students with not only an internationalized curriculum, but expanded opportunities for and the encouragement of the study of foreign languages, and the opportunity to develop a heightened understanding of other cultures. The internationalized university prepares students for employment and citizenry in an interdependent world.

The presence of international students is a key component in any campus's attempt to internationalize itself. It is one aspect of internationalization which is already occurring in most institutions. An institution may wish to change the number of international students on its campus, their geographic distribution, graduate/undergraduate ratio, or how these students are integrated into campus life. But their presence is a critical first step in internationalization.

But more important is the benefit international students provide to U.S. institutions in their efforts to internationalize, to educate students, to prepare for the challenges of the next century. International students contribute in several ways: by providing cultural diversity; by sharing their values, life experiences and world views; by serving as resources in the creation of a more cosmopolitan learning environment; and, of course, by achieving laudatory scholarship and study in classrooms, laboratories, and libraries. By their presence, international students enable the entire university community — faculty, staff, U.S. students, and other internationals — to prepare itself for global interdependence.

Traditionally, universities have had varied success in realizing the potential benefit resulting from enrolling international students. Many individual students, faculty, and staff have benefitted tremendously from their interactions with international students. Many academic departments have been influenced by the contributions, to their academic disciplines and to an expanded world view for study in the disciplines, of international students and scholars. Some institutions have been able to develop programmatic activities that more fully utilize the abundant educational opportunities provided by the presence of international students. However, organized institutional efforts have been, as discussed in Chapter 6, by no means the norm.

This failure to adequately integrate international students into campus life and the fabric of the university educational experience is at least in part an outgrowth of how the provision of student services for international students has been viewed. The traditional model has viewed international students as a discrete, specialized clientele, and then assigned primary responsibility for this client group to the designated foreign student adviser/office on campus. And, while such assignment has come in part as a positive recognition of the special and unique needs of international students, it also, all too often, has meant that other aspects of student services have not been encouraged to respond to international students as their own clientele.

At the same time, historically, little emphasis has been placed on the value of international education for American students. International education has been frequently defined as something U.S. institutions do to foreigners, not something that occurs interactively for U.S. and international students. Encouraging international education for American students has been largely the domain of certain academic departments or faculty and, in fact, most study abroad offices are located administratively within academic units. International education, occurring through study abroad, internationalized curriculum, or enhanced opportunity for cultural diversity by means of interaction with international students, has not been widely viewed as a critical aspect of student development. And yet for internationalization of our institutions to succeed, student affairs professionals must be asked to assume active roles as international educators. For their positions, expertise, and involvement with students' lives make them, in fact, key personnel in the internationalization process.

In the preceding chapters, the authors have touched upon the special needs of international students and the challenges student affairs professionals face in meeting these special needs. Yet, these authors also show that these needs can be effectively addressed within the student services arena and that substantial expertise exists to do so.

It is not sufficient to remand the care of and service to international students to the international student services office on campus. Neither is it satisfactory to provide services within our areas without considering the special needs of this clientele or the internationalization goals of our institutions. Rather, it is crucial to recognize that the expertise for providing appropriate services to this portion of our clientele rests not only with international student advisers, but also with our residence hall directors, health care providers, admissions counselors, leadership trainers, and other professionals within student affairs.

Successful integration of international students into the campus community and, as a result, internationalization of the campus, can occur in many different ways that can be affected by student affairs professionals. A first step toward internationalization is the integration of international students into the mainstream student culture.

An important task for student services is the generation of a better mixture of international and American students in most aspects of campus life. Opportunities for enhanced interaction include the areas of leadership development, committee membership, peer advising programs, on-campus employment opportunities, roommate and residence hall assignments, resident hall adviser employment, student organizations, and student government.

It is by working in concert and by incorporating international students into the mainstream student clientele that it is possible to utilize the presence of international students on our campuses to create an international learning environment. Thus, student affairs professionals are able to provide a nurturing environment for international students within the framework of student development. Just as important is the creation of an international learning environment for American students who must also learn and grow and prepare for life in an interdependent world.

For those involved with the provision of student services, it is easy, in the rush of providing basic services, dealing with crises and meeting deadlines, to forget or downplay their roles as educators. But student affairs professionals are, in fact, both educators and international educators. Thus it is, in no small part, their responsibility to prepare students to grapple with the momentous concerns of the 21st century.

These students, American and international, will face serious challenges in their roles as chemists, engineers, government leaders, philosophers, and, even, educators in an increasingly interdependent world. Those working with students are also challenged, as it is their task to prepare students for the 21st century. Thus do they meet their challenge as educators and an international educators. It is an exciting challenge, indeed.

References

Harari, M. (1981). *Internationalizing the curriculum and the campus: Guidelines for AASCU institutions.* Washington, D.C.: American Association of State Colleges and Universities.

Southern Governors Association (1986). *International education: Cornerstone of competition.* The report of the Southern Governors' Association Advisory Council on International Education.

Lambert, R.D. (1989). *International studies and the undergraduate.* Washington, D.C.: American Council on Education.

APPENDIX

ADDITIONAL RESOURCES

Publications

Burak, P.A. (1987). *Crisis management in a cross-cultural setting.* Washington, D.C.: National Association for Foreign Student Affairs.

Helman, C. (1985). *Culture, health and illness: An introduction for health professionals.* Littleton, MA: PSG Publishing Co., Inc.

International student health: A special issue. *Journal of American College Health,* 36, 6.

Karel, S.; Naughton, J.; and Stockert, N. (1986). *Health care for the international student: Asia and the Pacific.* Washington, D.C.: National Association for Foreign Student Affairs.

National Association for Foreign Student Affairs (1988). *The risks and realities of health insurance: A guide for advisers to foreign students and scholars.* Washington, D.C.: author.

Other Resources

HealthLink. Washington, D.C.: National Association for Foreign Student Affairs.
This computer-based clearinghouse within the National Association of Foreign Student Affairs (NAFSA) contains international student health information and resources from

campuses and organizations in the United States. It includes information on products (e.g., international student health handbooks, translated health brochures), policies (e.g., health insurance and immunization policies at various institutions and how these are enforced), and program (e.g., model health orientation programs, discussion groups for spouses, workshops on stress management).

Your health in the United States (1981). Columbus, Ohio: Ohio University.

This videotape accompanies a workbook and sets of brochures in English, Spanish, Chinese, and Arabic. Both the videotape and brochures can be used in orienting international students to the U.S. health care system. Developed by Ohio University, the video provides a general introduction to the types of health care facilities, professionals, and procedures in the United States. The brochures provide translations of basic medical terminology.

NASPA Publications
ORDER FORM

	Quantity	Cost

Puzzles and Pieces in Wonderland:
The Promise and Practice of
Student Affairs Research.
$7.95 members, $9.95 nonmembers   _____ _____

The Role of Student Affairs in
Institution-Wide Enrollment
Management Strategies.
$7.95 members, $9.95 nonmembers   _____ _____

The Invisible Leaders: Student
Affairs Mid-manager.
$7.95 members, $9.95 nonmembers   _____ _____

The New Professional: A Resource
Guide for New Student Affairs
Professionals and Their
Supervisors.
$7.95 members, $9.95 nonmembers   _____ _____

From Survival to Success:
Promoting Minority Student
Retention.
$7.95 members, $9.95 nonmembers   _____ _____

Student Affairs and Campus
Dissent.
$5.95 members, $7.50 nonmembers   _____ _____

Alcohol Policies and Procedures on
College and University Campuses.
$5.95 members, $7.50 nonmembers   _____ _____

	Quantity	Cost

Opportunities for Student
Development in Two-Year
Colleges.
$5.95 members, $7.50 nonmembers   _____ _____

Private Dreams, Shared Visions:
Student Affairs Work in Small
Colleges.
$5.95 members, $7.50 nonmembers   _____ _____

Translating Theory into Practice:
Implications of Japanese
Management Theory for Student
Personnel Administrators.
$5.95 members, $7.50 nonmembers   _____ _____

Risk Management and the Student
Affairs Professional.
$5.95 members, $7.50 nonmembers   _____ _____

Career Perspectives in Student
Affairs.
$5.95 members, $7.50 nonmembers   _____ _____

Points of View.
$5 members, $7 nonmembers   _____ _____

TOTAL   _____ _____

Please return completed form with check, money order, or credit card authorization. Return to: NASPA, 1875
Connecticut Avenue, NW, Suite 418, Washington, D.C. 20009-5728; (202) 265-7500.

Payment enclosed ☐   Bill my credit card ☐

VISA ☐   MasterCard ☐   Expiration Date _____

Account Number _____ Signature _____

Please Print

Name _____ NASPA Membership ID No. _____

Address _____

City _____ State _____ Zip _____